SELF-SABOTAGE?

What **it is**,
Why **we do it**,
When **we do it**,
How **to Overcome It!**

Cris Baker

LEADERS IN GLOBAL PUBLISHING

Published by Motivational Press, Inc.

2360 Corporate Circle

Suite 400

Henderson, NV 89074

www.MotivationalPress.com

Manufactured in the United States of America.

ISBN: 978-1-62865-030-3

This book:

Self-Sabotage? What it is, Why we do it, When we do it How to Overcome It!

is copyright. We encourage you to obtain your own personal copy by visiting our website at:

www.LifeStrategies.net/ssm1

Contents

O INITIAL STUFF

0.1   Acknowledgments

Many, many people both deserve and have my full appreciation for their assistance over many years to making this manuscript possible. Family, friends, colleagues, and clients have all made major contributions. It would not have been possible without them.

Thank you to the whole of my long-suffering family, who were the first to bear the brunt of my many failures. They were the guinea-pigs in my initial attempts to learn how to function as a real human being. I started realizing the difference between what works, and what doesn't, at a very tender age.

Thank you to my numerous teachers, who have all made an enormous contribution to my life. Included among them are Edward de Bono, Alexander Everett, Byron Katie, Robert Kiyosaki, Anthony Robbins, and M. Scott Peck. Many were especially tolerant and actually welcomed me and my many questions back for a second and even a third course. Their books have also provided many hours of incisive reading. The many who I have had the temerity to exclude, please excuse me, it's not that I don't appreciate your invaluable contribution, it's rather that as I get older, my clarity about past events diminishes. I freely confess that I cannot remember anywhere near a fraction of the courses I've been on and the many wonderful teachers who I regret not being able to name individually . Thank you all anyway.

Apart from many excellent courses, I have read hundreds of books which have given me literally thousands of insights and advances in personal growth. To name just a few, Richard Bach, Deepak Chopra, Wayne Dyer, David Hawkins, Osho Rajneesh, and Neale Donald Walsch have all provide me with innumerable insights. It would be impossible to list all the authors who have contributed so much to my personal development, so I'm not going to even attempt it. This, fortuitously, also lets my memory off the hook. This does not mean that I am not truly appreciative of those who have made such efforts to write clearly. Their clarity ensured I have not only understood what they are saying, but actually used some of their insights to my personal benefit. This book itself has benefitted from the wisdom shown by you all, thank you for providing such a great model to follow.

My clients also have contributed immensely to this book, and have sometimes been unwitting guinea-pigs as I learnt the full truth of that wonderful idiom - fail your way to success. Of course, I should point out that all names have been changed to protect the innocent. You know who you are.

Last but not least, my colleague Vic Johnson was the initial inspiration for this book. His idea was for me to write something that would inspire people to stop their self-sabotage and thereby improve their lives. To the extent that this book successfully accomplishes this challenging task, the credit goes to him. All failings in this regard are, of course, mine and mine alone.

●- - - - - - - ●- - - - - - - - - - ●- - - - - - - ●- - - - - - ●

0.2   Editor's preface

A wise man once said, "Today is the first day of the rest of your life." So very true. But is your life fulfilling you? How may people have consciously chosen to live happy, well-balanced, and fulfilling lives?

A truly rewarding life is very different to mere existence. And you want to become more effective at creating the life you really want to live, I guess that's why you picked up this book, right? Who wouldn't want a happy, well-balanced, and fulfilling life, one that leaves you feeling complete at the end of each day?

You'll find some simple stories here, mostly of undesirable experiences, along with the benefits to be drawn about making more out of life. It's your choice whether or not to take advantage of what lies within these pages. This is an introduction, a start on some different perspectives, different ways of looking at things which can give you more personal power.

Some people think this sounds too good to be true. Are you asking yourself, what's the catch? Rest assured, there is no catch. This book will show you how you can change any undesirable outcomes in your life and get your life working for you — rather than against you. Here you will see what to change, but only you can make it happen. It really is as simple as that.

Are you just looking for temporary relief from an unsatisfactory situation, or do you want a permanent cure? Despite what they tell themselves, many people merely want superficial relief because they are not prepared to put in the hard work, dedication and effort required to implement a cure. Then they stay where they are, and continue to be dissatisfied with what's happening in their lives. Some even complain about the circumstances!

Some primary questions to ponder are:

- Are you hungry and humble?

- Hungry enough to invest the necessary time and energy?

- Hungry for the results that are within your reach from effort on this path?

- Do you recognize that what you know has got you this far, and that to progress further, you're going to have to learn something different?

Some of the changes may make you feel uncomfortable, but if you have the courage not to give up, if you really want the benefits of a truly fulfilling life, then overcoming self-sabotage is paramount.

When you understand that your circumstances are the consequences of your choices thus far, you will be ready and able to change them. Only when you do get this simple truth can you see beyond what you know at this moment to yet more powerful perspectives that have been hidden from you. With an open mind, you can use these to achieve more desirable circumstances. So change perspective! In reality you can't expect to look at different things if you don't change the way you look at things.

Self-sabotage hinders your success. The material you will find within these pages will help free your mind, allowing you to produce different results. Through these pages, you will begin to understand the self-sabotage phenomenon, empowering you toward a better life. This tried and tested way gives you more out of life, and more satisfaction, more harmony in your life .

1 THE TRUTH BEHIND FALSEHOOD

1.1 What Qualifies Me to Write this Book

"Experience is that marvelous thing that enables you to recognize a mistake when you make it again."
- Franklin P. Jones

I would love to open by telling you that I always learn a lesson from one of my mistakes the first time around. But I can't tell you that - it's not true! In fact, I have made some of the same mistakes over and over again.

Rarely do I do things right the first time around. For that matter, the second time is usually not much better. Okay, I'll be honest! I have screwed up so many times, I've stopped counting. I ran out of fingers and toes at a really early age!

Let me share another secret: I like things to be exactly the way I want them to be. Maybe you know someone else like this, maybe even intimately! I want what I want when I want it, and if in the past I didn't get it, I could get a tad upset. Snatch and grab may be the law in the animal kingdom - but for us humans? Nope, I found out instead that *gasp* we're actually expected to consider other people in our civilized society.

Let's see. Relationships? I'm embarrassed to tell you how many failed ones I've had, don't even ask.

Jobs? Ditto. Let it suffice to say that I've been fired five times, including the time I was handed the pink slip *before* I even started work! That was a great morale booster, let me tell you. I was working on a farm, a summer job picking hops, and the owner wanted someone to employ people for the following season. "Would you advertise for me and make it happen?" he asked. "Sure, I'll do it," I replied, although I was not at all sure what to do, I'd never done anything similar before. He must have picked up on this, because a couple of days later, he told me thanks, but no thanks - he had already found someone else!

A mind that thinks a hundred good ideas all at the same time? Yes, indeed, and

I believed each one was true, whether or not it had any basis in reality! My mind used to run around in circles. I actually used to believe I've thought it, so it must be true - in my own infallibility. Arrogance? Maybe (okay, you got me. It's arrogance).

If that were not enough, I actually had the audacity to believe that my own personal view of the world was totally accurate. Yet facts are facts, and so when we disagree how can we both be right? It took a long, long while to realize that disagreement about facts is a problem also caused by arrogance. And what's a long, long while, you ask? No, dinosaurs were not roaming the earth, but it was *blush* decades - yes, in the plural.

"They" sometimes say that control is indispensable, and indeed it is. But, for me, this didn't mean control over my own thoughts, my words, and my deeds. It meant control over other people and their behavior. *If only they'd do it my way, the world would be a better place and we'd all be happy* was the mantra to live by. It was my way or the highway. See the vanity here? I thought I knew better than *they* did how to run *their* lives, and what *they* should do. Just how had humanity managed to survive this long without my opinions and advice?

Make lemonade out of lemons

Many of these experiences enabled me to recognize my mistakes as I made them again. They also allowed me to distill strategies that do bear fruit. How's that for making lemonade out of lemons? Although the lemonade did not squeeze itself.

On the path of self-improvement, I came to my senses. I understood, for example, that we can't all be right, all the time, about everything. Many of you know this already, but for me it was an amazing revelation. I thought, "I don't know how to do this," meant "this can't be done." Yet, "It can't be done" does not mean "it" can't be done at all. It only means that *I* don't know how to do it. Humility at its finest. It had finally dawned on me that being happy was more enjoyable than being right.

Clearly, I am no stranger to mistakes and disasters of all kinds. And all of these experiences qualify me to write this book. In other words, I have been tripping over my own erroneous beliefs for so long, and have been hurt by their consequences so frequently, that I have become an expert at discovering what *doesn't* work. You can bet the farm that it was extremely embarrassing, not to mention painful more often that I care to admit as I helplessly watched another seemingly good idea bite the dust.

Here's the deal: I want you to benefit from my mistakes. Simplify your life by outsourcing your failures to an expert! Why suffer personally when you can sit in the comfort of your own home and experience the consequences of failure vicariously?

No bumps, no bruises. Read and laugh aloud at the many stupid things I've done, watch as the world hits me on the head again to drive a very obvious point home. As you wipe away the tears of laughter, you'll think, "Man, I'm not going to make THAT mistake..."

All kidding aside, if I can pick myself up by my bootstraps, dust myself off, and learn from my errors, so can you. If you have an open mind and the right attitude, *you,* too, can learn from *my* mistakes. This, I do know.

I like people with a great attitude, and one of my favorites is Thomas Alva Edison. Before he succeeded in inventing a viable light bulb, he reportedly tried and failed five thousand times. He was later asked whether failing so many times had discouraged him.

His response?

"Fail? I didn't fail. I was just very successful in finding out what didn't work. Eventually, I found out what did."

And *that* is the very thing I want to share with you today. Want to find out what does work? Well then, print this out, grab yourself a cup of coffee, curl up in your favorite spot, ignore all distractions, and start turning the pages!

• - - - - - - • - - - - - - - • - - - - - - • - - - - - •

1.2 Is it true? Or self-deception again?

"What should I do," I asked myself, while standing in the corner. I was just seven-years-old and in the second grade. This was my first real dilemma.

The teacher had gone out of the classroom, instructing us not to talk. We ignored her. Along with a bunch of other children I was whispering.

A little while later, the teacher came back into the room. She singled me out, "I heard you talking as I came into the room. Why were you talking when I told you not to talk?" she asked me, ignoring all the others who had been talking as well.

"But I wasn't talking," I replied. This was factually correct. As she came into the room, I wasn't talking. I had been talking maybe thirty seconds earlier, but not when she came into the room.

"You're lying," she said, and my punishment was to stand in the corner. "You can come back to your seat only when you admit that you haven't told the truth."

What should I do, I wondered? I knew I was telling the truth, but she wanted me to lie. What felt like hours later, but perhaps amounted to only thirty minutes, I was still there.

Eventually, I worked it out in my head: I would tell her what she wanted to hear, even though it was untrue. "Yes, I did lie."

The teacher later told my mother that she had caught her child lying. My mother assumed the teacher was referring to another sibling, since she knew I was always truthful. She was amazed when she found out it was me. "What really happened?" my mother asked me afterward.

"It wasn't me. The teacher made a mistake, she thought I was talking, but I wasn't," I replied.

Although we disagreed with each other, technically both the teacher and I were right. Yet, seen with different perspectives, we were also both wrong.

· - - - - - · - - - - - ·

Truth and Effectiveness

This book is actually a very down-to-earth exploration of truth and effectiveness. It's about the self-sabotage mechanism (ssm) with its ardor for deception. Many of us already realize that self-sabotage is a dead-end street. It takes us where we do not want to be - such as the corner in the classroom!

What is self-sabotage? How does it work? Who does it affect? When can we see it in action, and where does it take us? These are such fundamental questions to reflect upon!

The ssm's job is to hinder our progress, to lead us down the wrong path, and bring us what we don't want to be, do, or have. If it were truly honest, none of us would continue to let it any say in our lives. But it's not that easy - it's a master of deceit, trickery, and evasion.

Many people, perhaps most all of us, allow ourselves to be deceived to some degree. Whether the falsehood is small or large, we are still misled in some way. This means that our view of what has happened, or what is now, is inaccurate or incomplete in some manner. As I found out in the second grade, all actions have consequences. And some consequences are more desirable than others.

Deception and falsehood are not truth, nor are they the opposite of truth. Just as darkness is the absence of light - rather than its opposite - falsity is the absence of truth. This is a crucial distinction which, by giving no recognition to deception, gives it no power.

Now, some say that truth is personal, different for each individual, and my truth may not be your truth. Yes, perspectives and meanings are individual. Yet facts, which are external, are not necessarily the same as our internal take on the matter. Facts are facts, they may be difficult to pin down, but they can be stated objectively. Whereas understanding and observations generally differ from one person to another. Our viewpoints, our personalities, and our interpretations also diverge; they may be close to someone else's but not identical. Yet this is not a metaphysical discussion, which we'll leave to the intellectuals and philosophers. Let's rather focus on the results that truth and falsehood bear in practice.

Nothing here is meant to suggest the self-sabotage mechanism is right, bad, or wrong. Or even that deceiving ourselves, or being deceived, is right, bad, or wrong. Although it won't get us where we want to be, and it's tough to get to get there without first knowing where we are now. The more inaccurate our picture of where we are, the more difficult it will be to plot a course to where we really want to be. Self-sabotage is just ineffective.

This book discusses a few common viewpoints which produce less desirable circumstances. The real job, the harder task is to learn to avoid these mistakes. By practicing these strategies, you'll become more effective, increase your personal power, and improve your future. Although you won't find much here about what to do![1]

Questions 1.2

1   *What is this book about?*

2   *How do deception and falsehood differ from truth?*

3.   *Is the self-sabotage mechanism right, bad, or wrong?*

• - - - - - - • - - - - - - - - - - • - - - - - - - • - - - - - - •

---

1 One of the major distinctions between Life Strategies and coaching is that most coaching seems to be about what to do - the content of your life - whereas we instead focus on your context. As Robert Kiyosaki sagely notes in Retire Young, Retire Rich,

"it is not so much what you do that makes you rich or poor. It is more the context surrounding what you do that makes you rich or poor. That is why when people ask me what I do or what I invest in I reply; 'Please don't ask me what I do. Ask me what I think about what I do.'"

1.3 Live The Life You'd Love To Live!

"Meditate," said the still small voice. I ignored it, as usual. I used to not pay much attention to my intuition, until one day I realized that whenever I did, it seemed to lead to undesirable consequences.

"Meditate!" it repeated, a little more insistently. This was unusual... my intuition rarely urges. In fact, the words "still" and "small" are very good descriptions of the way it operates.

Hmm, I thought, I've never meditated while driving before, what an idea!

The traffic lights at the bottom of the hill turned green, and then off we went. My car is quite fast, and I'd soon caught up with the traffic moving up the hill. So I switched to the empty inside lane to pass the slower vehicles.

As I sped around the bend at the top of the hill, a car was parked in the most dangerous spot - on the bridge just past the bend, a few yards before the road widened with a hard shoulder. It had its flashers on, but at the speed I was traveling I knew I could not stop in time.

I had no time to think what to do; my body acted on instinct, guiding the car into the space between the two vehicles in the outside lane. Since I was also driving faster than both of them, crashing into the rear of the one in front also seemed unavoidable.

Once I had passed the parked car, my reflexes then guided me back into the inside lane. My car made a couple of wiggles after the second violent lane change, and then we were safe.

"What happened?" I asked myself. As I thought about it, I broke into a cold sweat. Without the automatic responses of my body, there would have been a serious accident. I could even be dead!

• - - - - - • - - - - - •

Intuition

I'm just like many of you. I've been rich and I've been poor; overweight and slender. I've lived through good situations and bad ones; have been where I wanted to be, and where I didn't. And I've had seemingly miraculous experiences, and many far less desirable. This was one of the more miraculous ones, and all of them, good and bad, have taught me that my intuition, my still small voice is definitely on my side.

Living the life we all want to live is amazingly simple. We all want whatever we want to be, do, or have. So just do what works to get it; Don't do what doesn't work! This magic formula always works, because of its focus on both results and the effectiveness of our actions. It's your job just to observe honestly - without self-sabotage - what does work for you and what doesn't.

Yet if this is true, how come so many of us are dissatisfied in life or unhappy to some extent? What's the problem?

Does this simple formula really work? If so, why doesn't it work for all of us? And if this simple plan does work, why don't we work this plan? Can it really be that easy?

No. It's not always easy. And this answer gives us one of the problems, so many of us think that simple means easy!

But it doesn't. And this confusion is one of the reasons we can find life unsatisfactory. The simple is often very difficult! And just why is it very difficult so often?

Many of us haven't yet worked out that we have a self-sabotage mechanism, which can and does hijack the mind. When it does, our thoughts are no longer reliable even though we may be absolutely sure we're right! Some thoughts are true and yet sometimes, a thought is untrue. As Mark Twain powerfully observed,

> *"It ain't what you don't know that gets you into trouble. It's what you know for sure that just ain't so.*

Our own thoughts can lead us down the garden path! We have to learn to distinguish the true thoughts from the fallacious ones. Simple, right? Yes indeed, yet - again - simple does not mean easy. It's actually harder than it might sound, but once you start practicing this skill, it can transform your life!

That's right. Our thinking can be an unreliable guide to getting what we want and to where we want to be. Yet we don't think to explore the validity of our thoughts, even when the lack of real results tells us clearly that we do have a problem somewhere.

Clarity in thinking is primary. The less clarity, the more we tend to deceive ourselves. And how many of us have stopped to realize that self-deception is a reliable guide to achieving just one thing? What we don't want!

How can anyone be expected to choose an effective path if they are confused about where they are now?

Questions 1.3

1   *What is the Magic Pill that gives you whatever you want to be, do, or have; no matter what it is.*

2   *Are there any other incisive strategies to help you get wherever you want to be?*

3   *Why is clarity in thinking vital?*

• - - - - - - • - - - - - - • - - - - - - • - - - - - - •

1.4   Every Perspective has Some Personal Power

Everything we consider to be true is just our perspective. In contrast to an external fact, our truth is an individual experience, a consequence not only of the content but also of our internal context; It's our take on the matter. And sometimes we find that others do not share our perspective.

Every perspective is just one of many, each having more (or less) power than another, and which may contradict the way we currently see things. Generally, the more different the perspective is, the bigger the difference in power will be.

If you are in San Francisco and you drive south, you come to Los Angeles. If you were in San Diego, however, driving south will not get you to Los Angeles, you'd need to drive north. You may know that you're in the USA, and even that you're in Southern California. Yet without knowing accurately where you are now, driving south won't get you where you want to be.

There's nothing wrong with driving south - but it's an ineffective course of action that won't get you to your goal. And that's what's fundamental - being effective. We all hold various viewpoints in life. Some perspectives work well for us, and others don't.

Our assessment that driving south is not working doesn't suggest that this is wrong per se, even though it won't get us to our desired destination. Denying error stops us from getting to the truth, even though denial is often more comfortable than change. Truth can indeed be frightening, as Dr. David Hawkins puts it:

"Enslavement by illusion is comfortable; it is the liberation by Truth that people fear."

Live in the contradiction

Robert Kiyosaki, the author of the book "Rich Dad, Poor Dad", tells the story about listening to a tape by a real-estate expert. Halfway through, the expert said something that contradicted what Robert knew to be true. This doesn't make sense, Robert thought, and he rewound the tape to listen again. It still didn't make sense to him, but Robert was open-minded. So he kept listening to the same segment. A while later, he had finally managed to work out the perspective from which the expert was coming.

Robert went on to say that this shift in perspective had made him millions of dollars over the years. But what really made him those extra millions was his willingness to continue listening to what seemed wrong.

To increase our personal power, we need to be willing to look carefully at new perspectives, even if this means we have to be willing to live in the contradiction. Until we open ourselves to a new perspective, we will not understand it, it may then come across to us as "wrong."

So we live in the uncertainty - in the dilemma - until we come to understand a new point of view. Robert Kiyosaki only made those extra millions because he was willing to explore what seemed wrong. Only then can we see the extra power that a change in context holds for us. We need to be open-minded. Why, you may wonder, is this so vital?

When we are being right, our mind closes to the possibility of another opinion also being right, and our context is negative. The resultant negative emotions, such as disagreement, and frustration, tend to stop us from looking openly at what will indeed seem wrong - each and every new perspective...

Yet, as so many have observed over the ages, if we cannot quieten our negative minds, how will we ever learn? When will we become free? If we do not change, then nothing will change. As Antoine De Saint-Exupery so astutely observed:

"What saves a man is to take a step. Then another step."

Questions 1.4

1   *Since facts are facts, why don't other people share our truths?*

2   *What's crucial about accuracy?*

3   *What enabled Robert Kiyosaki to gain millions of dollars from that real-estate tape.*

• - - - - - • - - - - - • - - - - - • - - - - - •

1.5   For Real Achievement - Learn the Rules

Our goal here is to empower you to create your life the way you really want it. A major problem is that what people think they want is often not what they really want. What you think you want may have been determined by your ssm, rather than the real you. Some people haven't yet decided what they want in life, and the ssm may try to tell them this itself is a problem. Yet we all really want to live the life we'd love to live. So how do we get to do that? Well, read on...

First, it's essential to understand what's happening:

- Who's involved in the process of creation?

- What's involved in gaining, or regaining, more power over your life?

- How have the results you have achieved so far been achieved?

- When do you sabotage yourself?

- Why are your circumstances the way they are?

- Where is the seat of power in your life?

- Which laws of life govern the results you are experiencing?

The power to improve all aspects of your situation comes through learning new perspectives, in changing your context, exploring truth, beliefs, and self-sabotage. As you develop more clarity about the rules of life, what's happening and why, you become more effective at creating the outcomes you really want - such as joy, even in challenging circumstances. This clarity in our thinking processes is vital to achieving the real success that's actually possible...

In this book we'll explore the universal self-sabotage mechanism which we all have. Since the ssm will no doubt attempt to sabotage your exploration, it may take you quite a while to understand just how much self-sabotage affects all of our lives and how to cope with it. How long this takes will be determined by the time and effort you put into studying its very different perspectives and your dedication to practicing suggested strategies. It will also depend on how well you handle all the distractions and temptations which will arise as you learn the rules. Many years ago, Sir Francis Bacon observed this so very beautifully:

"Nature, to be commanded, must be obeyed."

Questions 1.5

1.   *What do we suggest as indispensable here?*

2.   *When might you not know what you really want?*

3.   *How do you gain the power to improve all aspects of your situation?*

• - - - - - • - - - - - - • - - - - - • - - - - - •

1.6   How to read this book

Some people read a book from cover to cover, others of us like to dip in and explore. So we've broken down some different perspectives, powerful viewpoints about life and understanding how it works, into what we call koans. What are koans, and what purpose do they serve? Simply put, koans increase your ability to manage your context, your internal world. At Life Strategies, we use the word koan to mean a particular perspective. A distinction. Another viewpoint. A different way of looking at an incident, a situation, or even a phrase. Many feel a surge of energy when they first understand - "get" - a koan , that's a foretaste of the increase in inner power available.

Now when you do more than just understand a koan - when you really know it - you can use the extra strength inherent in its new perspective. So you need to have each koan come alive for you (there are many - hundreds). Once you have invested the time and energy so that it lives for you, you can harness its strength.

By realizing the inner strength inherent in a koan you become more creative, more capable, and more effective. We've all heard that "Knowledge is power." We bring that phrase to life, by enabling you to access that power.

Each koan, each perspective is designed to be free-standing, to be read by itself. They can be enjoyed independently to help us make the often challenging differentiation between fact and fallacy. Some will undoubtedly differ from our personal or social opinions, which only goes to show that common human beliefs can often be the exact opposite of the underlying truth. Belief is a barrier to authentic knowing!

Some people may find difficulties with various viewpoints, while others will have no problem. Remember that we first learn to drive in a parking lot, leaving all complexities such as any other traffic until we're competent with the basics. So take these new perspectives slowly, ignore the ssm's desire to deal with the more complex implications immediately. To start with, be gentle with yourself and your expectations. Enjoy exploring these ideas even if some of your long-held illusions are challenged. Many of the apparent disparities resolve themselves upon mature reflection, so please remain open-minded.

For your circumstances to improve, you'll find it valuable to reflect on these questions:

- Have you a tendency to self-sabotage which exaggerates the often irrelevant details that divide people? Or

- Would you rather emphasize the central point of truth which unites us, although this requires both integrity and courage?

- Do you recognize that truth, rather than illusion or error, is real? That untruth having no reality just leads to more and more untruth.

- Are you among the third or so of all people who are really interested in truth for its own sake? And find happily that truth leads to truth.

We don't believe in believing

None of the viewpoints suggested here is to be taken as gospel. Please don't believe any of them unquestioningly; in fact don't believe anything from anybody without question! Check out everything you hear and see to find out what works for you in the context of your own experience. Results are the criterion here - not your beliefs. And since you're reading this book, I trust you're willing to do this already.

We're simple realists, we don't believe in believing! If you believe, it's because you don't know. When you know something to be true, belief that it's true is unnecessary. This is all about questioning the thoughts that your mind believes - or other people want you to adopt - and instead coming to what you know to be your truth. Don't just accept the words of experts simply because of their status as experts. Don't delegate any of your thinking, especially to the ssm!

In reading something new here, sometimes your heart may dance joyfully, or it'll start singing new music as it sees how well this fits! You will then know, before you think about it, that what you've found is your truth, even though you may recognize that you don't necessarily understand it fully yet! This internal song and dance, this fragrance of rightness, is an indication of the extra personal power available to you here. So don't ignore this feeling, instead invest some serious energy and make that increase in personal power your own! More personal power goes hand in hand with your ability to create.

No one changes anything unless he or she sees that there's a benefit to change. We all need to realize that relying on error just makes us less effective. Compared to the undesirable consequences that mistakes tend to bring, desirable ones are well, er ... more desirable.

"Minds are like parachutes; they work best when open."
 - Lord Thomas Dewar

Questions 1.6

1.   What is a koan?

2.   Why is it paramount that you do more than just understand a koan?

3.   How will the self-sabotage mechanism deal with all this?

4.   Is what is written here to be taken as gospel?

• - - - - - - • - - - - - - - - - - • - - - - - - • - - - - - •

2 IF AT FIRST YOU DON'T SUCCEED

2.1   The Enemy of Success - self-sabotage

Many of us find that although we know what we need to do, sometimes, we just don't do it. Our best intentions can be sabotaged by circumstances, by various events, or even by laziness. And it takes real honesty and clarity to see that we have had a part in creating those circumstances. The self-sabotage mechanism much prefers us to see self-sabotage in our friends and relatives than in ourselves. After all, if we see our own, we'd have to acknowledge our own imperfections, and who wants to do that? It's safer to see only others as imperfect, right?

What we're running up against here is the self-sabotage mechanism (ssm). Everybody has one, and it's working all the time – it never takes a vacation or a day off. Its function – as the name suggests – is to sabotage and hence prevent our progress. Since the ssm enables us to experience the rough with the smooth, how can it be wrong, but it can be rather frustrating! As the insightful saying goes,

"It takes the bitter and the sweet to make life complete!"

It's no secret that we would much rather experience pleasant and enjoyable circumstances. Most of us prefer to avoid the arduous as well as the painful. Yet all actions have consequences, and some consequences are more desirable than others. So in this book we explore proven strategies to create more of the former and less of the latter.

To do this, we need to invest the time and effort into getting a clear handle on the self-sabotage mechanism.

- What is it?

- Who does it affect?

- How does it do what it does?

- When is it in operation?

- Why do we have one anyway?

- Where can we see it in action?

- Which strategies can we follow to stop it from running our lives?

The self-sabotage mechanism actually rejects what is true because truth denies its methodology of deception. Reality is empowered by credibility, while self-sabotage lacks integrity, consistency, and will even attempt to label what is true as falsehood.

The ssm will attempt to persuade you to reject these powerful perspectives because it wants you to believe only its own perspectives. However, the path to real success is simple. Don't live in denial, stop projecting your own instincts onto others, and take responsibility for all your actions and especially for their consequences. The necessary commitment to truth required may be easier said than done. In the short-term, the consequences may not be that appealing. Yet, the stronger your dedication to truth, the more success you will achieve in the long-term.

Learning to cope with the self-sabotage mechanism is, therefore, vital to our personal growth. The more we know about self-sabotage, the more successful we can be in avoiding its inevitable consequences, thus paving the way to happier and more fulfilling lives.

> *"The unintelligent will not learn from his own mistakes, but the intelligent can even learn from others' mistakes."*
> *- Osho*

Questions 2.1

1   *Who finds your self-sabotage easy to recognize?*

2   *When is the self-sabotage mechanism at work, and not at work?*

3   *Why does the self-sabotage mechanism do what it does?*

4   *What is true about every action?*

5   *How does the ssm work?*

• - - - - - - • - - - - - - • - - - - - - • - - - - •

2.2   How self-sabotage works

Everyone has a self-sabotage mechanism, including me, you, your partner, friends, family, neighbors, and co-workers. It doesn't like to be seen, and it doesn't like change. As you start to improve your understanding of how life really works, the ssm will step up its efforts to ruin any progress you've made. I bet it's got you thinking, why on earth would you learn from my mistakes when you can make your own? Well, it's lots less painful!

The mission of this book is to help you become aware of the rules of life which affect the results you have created so far. If you are truly satisfied with what you have accomplished and where you are now, stick with what you're doing. Obviously, whatever you are doing is working wonders for you. If, on the other hand, the results are NOT what you want them to be, change! Only change will enable you to create what you really want in the future.

Insisting what you already know is right

A common self sabotage strategy is to insist that what you already know is right - which implies that exploring what you don't yet know would be a waste of time. At one time or another, most people have given into the temptation of being right - the stubborn urge to hold onto beliefs and activities that may no longer serve them. As you move through life, you carry with you all the beliefs and perspectives you have been holding onto, thus making any move or change more difficult. The larger, the heavier the belief you are attached to, the more likely it is to weigh you down and hinder you from moving forward.

Another perspective is not just different, it's. . .

The ssm may insist another perspective is wrong, rather than just different. So, even when you know that your mind can and does deceive you, it may continue to insist it is right! It may even start doubting your internal conclusions about tomorrow's results being more important than any discomfort you may be feeling today. (Think seriously, very seriously, about this one!)

Questioning your progress or your current path

The ssm may also question your path forward, or the progress you've already made just in starting something. This may help explain why so many people fail to continue with an exercise regiment they have already started. Think of the number of people who start a diet only to find themselves unhappily weighing the same or more a year later. What about the many smokers who try to stop, abandon their efforts and then rationalize their inability to quit this compelling though unhealthy habit. (How come I know this one so very well? See If it's simple, it must be easy, in Chapter Three.) Progress is made the second you start to make a change, but then that pesky ssm intervenes.

Negative emotions

When you begin to see how unreliable your thoughts can be, you also start to see the many other tricks that the self-sabotage mechanism has up its sleeve. It can create negative emotions about your actions and progress, or even about what you are exploring here in these pages. A powerful new perspective can evoke feelings of irritation and doubt, until you realize that all such negativity is the ssm trying to sabotage your progress. (Note the censorship in these here words - this is a family oriented publication!)

Just like a weight reduction program or an exercise regimen, any new path needs to be given a chance and time to produce results. Getting to understand the ssm can take a while, depending how aware you are to start with of its methods and its effect on your circumstances.

Impatient at repetition, or the apparent lack of immediate results?

Negative occurrences are best experienced vicariously. After all, why would you want to engage in something negative when someone else can relate their negative experiences from which you can learn? But the positive, you'd rather enjoy in person, that's just human nature. You enjoy beautiful flowers in the spring, the warmth of a lovely summer evening, brilliant fall colors in autumn, and warm fires in winter. Both nature and life repeat themselves endlessly. The point here is that impatience at repetition, and the seeming lack of immediate results, are common self-sabotage strategies. Rather, spend your time enjoying these wonderful experiences, and congratulate yourself instead on choosing to miss the many negative experiences you find related here.

Some twenty years ago, I decided to run a marathon. It seemed like a good idea at the time! I was already running over twenty miles a week, and the Runner's World training program I followed took over three months. It involved an hour's exercise most days and, toward the end, a twenty-mile run once a week. Doing all that exercise took both dedication and a lot of time. And yet the marathon itself was the most uncomfortable run I've ever had. I had a stitch in my side from ten miles out, and my girlfriend came in before me. This was the first time she'd run faster than me, or rather, that I'd run slower than her. I did finish, but it was only willpower that got me over the finish line.

Learning to cope effectively with the ssm is highly unlikely to take you less time than training to run a marathon. Like most worthwhile things, the more time you put in and the more energy you invest, the better the result! Although, initially, the task of becoming aware of your self-sabotage mechanism may be strenuously resisted, in the end you'll come out fit as a fiddle and won't even be out of breath.

> *"Courage is what it takes to stand up and speak; courage is also what it takes to sit down and listen."*
> *- Winston Churchill*

Questions 2.2

1 *When you start becoming aware of the self-sabotage mechanism, what happens?*

2 *What enables you to create what you really want for the future?*

3 *Why can a new perspective evoke feelings of irritation and doubt?*

4 *Do you need to personally experience all the negative as well as the positive aspects of life yourself?*

• - - - - - • - - - - - - • - - - - - - • - - - - - •

2.3   Are any of your thoughts stressful?

How much stress do you feel right now? The ssm may be at work trying to persuade you that everything you are learning here is wrong. Are your thoughts telling you that this book has little or no value for you whatsoever? If they are, your first job is to tell your ssm to be quiet and listen up!

It will try to persuade you that any perspective you don't agree with - or don't yet understand - is wrong. So don't fall into the trap of being right, an arrogant, not to mention totally erroneous, attitude. Don't immediately reject a new viewpoint just because it doesn't resonate with you. Explore it, make sure you understand it, check out what it can do for you. When you've finished exploring you can always go back to your current position if it holds no extra power for you, so by being open to a different viewpoint, you can't lose.

Each and every new perspective presents a possible new way of looking at a situation; which means that each one may have an increase in personal power for you. Keep in mind that you must remain open-minded to assess the value of anything. If you do find any value in a new viewpoint, that means it could improve your life. Then you have a decision to make which will, of course, have consequences.

We do not insist any of these perspectives are right, we merely suggest that each one is worth understanding.

There are thousands, even millions of ways of looking at life's different aspects. Here we take a few of the more basic ones that help us understand the ssm and present them in a form that is not too challenging. Our aim is to approach this subject in easily digestible, understandable steps to help us cope with it better. The ssm is very cunning, amazingly devious, and can and does use our rational and emotional capabilities against us!

"It is easy to be swept away by some overwhelming feeling... Depression, pain, and fear are gifts that say, 'Sweetheart, take a look at your thinking right now. You're living in a story that isn't true for you.' Living an untruth is always stressful."
- Byron Katie

Questions 2.3

1   *What causes some people to feel a little stressed by reading the ideas presented in this book?*

2   *How is each and every new perspective different?*

3   *Who always wins by exploring a new perspective?*

4   *Are there different ways of looking at any situation in life?*

5   *What does the ssm say about any perspective you don't agree with?*

• - - - - - - - • - - - - - - • - - - - - - - - • - - - - - •

2.4   Growing awareness

As you increase your awareness in life, you learn to avoid the ssm's more blatant strategies, and start to recognize some of its more subtle ones. This enables you to create with more ease, to have more of whatever you want to do, be, or have.

For most of us, learning what works - and what doesn't work - is an ever evolving task. Many people wait until the undesirable consequences have come along instead of assessing what might be effective to start with. By then, of course, it's often too late to turn back and do what works.

When you believe others without question, you probably assume they have our best interests at heart. This is optimistic at best and rather dangerous at worst. Yet how many people assume that the beliefs they have adopted so far in life really do serve them? Without investigation, are you wise to rely on the thoughts of others, or even on your own?

You're far better off when you learn to anticipate, to become more aware of the ssm and, ultimately, to overcome it. Increasing your awareness lets you know when you are sabotaging yourself, helps you avoid taking any action the ssm exhorts, and hence produces more desirable consequences. The ssm is against change, which is the only thing guaranteed in life — along with death and taxes, of course! Yet change is the only thing that can increase your personal power. This means inner change! If there's no change then nothing changes.

How do we know when the self-sabotage mechanism is involved or not? Very simple! When you want something; the ssm's job is to sabotage the process and instead bring you the opposite - what you don't like or don't want. So any time you are not completely happy with our circumstances - whenever you don't have exactly what you want - then the ssm is or has been involved somewhere along the way. Every time? Yes, to some extent, every time.

"The illiterate of the 21st century will not be those who cannot read and write, but those who cannot learn, unlearn, and relearn."
        - Alvin Toffler

Questions 2.4

1   *How does increasing your awareness help in life?*

2   *What is the point of learning to anticipate, to become aware of, and to cope better with the ssm?*

3   *Whenever you reach an undesirable consequence, what can you usually say is true?*

4   *How do you know when the ssm is involved?*

5   *In what way does the Alvin Toffler quote relate to the ssm as described here?*

2.5 Chunking down the problem

How do we begin to study such a vast subject as the self-sabotage mechanism and its many complex, subtle strategies? In business, we learn to break a problem down into smaller, more manageable parts, so we can resolve each part. Then we integrate everything back together into a coherent, rational whole.

This, of course, takes serious thinking. Thinking for yourself, rather than adopting other people's beliefs. It can be hard work to integrate new perspectives with those from your previous experiences. But it is, at the end of the day, such a worthwhile and enriching undertaking. It opens up new frontiers and widens your horizons. Growing your understanding is rather like growing a tree. It's an organic process, from the inside to the outside rather than from the external in. It's natural, and it can't be delegated. So don't be gullible, don't ignore this vital part of growing up, even though a favorite self-sabotage mechanism strategy is to persuade you to believe the contrary.

So in this book, we will follow the same proven strategy. We will break down the various different perspectives, the viewpoints about how life works, into what we call koans, as explained earlier, in How to read this book toward the end of the first chapter.

Your thoughts are not reliable

We will start with some simple koans. But as you now know, one of the very first facts about the ssm you'll encounter is that our thoughts are NOT a reliable guide to what's true for us. Sometimes the mind tells us the truth, and sometimes it doesn't. A very common ssm strategy is to hijack the mind, and use it to give us untruths. In a way, it's like internal brainwashing – getting us to subscribe to ideas that are false.

If you've ever made a mistake you probably did what you thought was right, even though it later turned out to be incorrect. I've made many more than one, as perhaps you already realize, how about you? Evaluating our mistakes shows us that some of our thinking is simply misleading - that it's been sabotaged. Because our thoughts are not reliable, each thought needs to be examined to see whether or not it is in fact true! This one perspective alone, if explored, understood, and integrated to become part of you - rather than just a dry, little-understood fact - will make a truly amazing difference to your life.

Your introduction to self-sabotage

This introduction to self-sabotage formally presents some koans. We'll start with some introductory viewpoints essential to increasing personal power. The subsequent chapter looks at the Law of Attraction, and explores some of its very different facets. Then we discuss various aspects of inner strength, how we think, and how we know what is and is not true for us. The next chapter gives us an introduction to coping with the ssm and how it tries to sabotage both our thoughts and our emotions to produce undesirable results or arduous situations in our lives.

So enjoy exploring these new perspectives. Some you will already know and some will be fresh. Whether or not you already understand them, or even find nothing new in them at all, the logical manner in which each koan is explained, and the carefully thought-out sequence of presentation will enhance your understanding and increase your inner power. And that's the real objective of the exercise: To permanently increase your inner power for the rest of your life, for you to become more effective.

As we observed earlier, it's simple to tell when the self-sabotage mechanism has been active. Every time we are not fulfilled in our circumstances that tedious ssm has probably been hard at work. And it may be busy trying to persuade you that this perspective itself is untrue. (In fact, it may be telling you right now that there's nothing of value in this book). So one of your fundamental tasks is to carefully investigate the ideas here, and see whether or not they hold any real value for you.

"There is no expedient to which a man will not resort to avoid the real labor of thinking."
- Sir Joshua Reynolds

Questions 2.5

1   *When you've made a mistake, what is probably true of your thoughts?*

2   *Who benefits when you evaluate your mistakes?*

3   *Why is it fundamental to evaluate each and every thought?*

• - - - - - - • - - - - - - • - - - - - - • - - - - - •

3 INCREASE YOUR PERSONAL POWER!

3.1   It's my thought, so it must be true!

"Call a plumber," said my still small voice, but my mind insisted, "I know I can do this, so why waste money calling a plumber? I can do this."

The kitchen sink was blocked in my Constantia home in Cape Town. I knew about unblocking sinks, I'd heard people talking about it. So, rather than waste money on a plumber, I got in the car and drove down to the hardware store to buy sink unblocking liquid. After pouring it into the sink, I read the instructions and found that I would have to leave it a while. It'll be clear tomorrow, I told myself.

In the morning, I checked on the sink to find it was still blocked. Yet why should I waste money on a plumber? I'm a strong, intelligent male, I can do it. Obviously the stuff wasn't strong enough, so I took another trip down to Constantia Village shopping center. "Please give me the strongest stuff you have," I requested of the clerk in the same hardware store.

Back at home, I knew what to do; open the tin, pour it down the sink, and leave it to work its magic. There was no need to read the instructions, I'd read them last time. So I opened the tin and just poured it down the sink!

The response was unanticipated. It reacted strongly with the previous unblocking liquid, and an explosion of acid immediately shot out of the hole. I was lucky my eyes weren't directly in the line of fire. It burnt big holes in my shirt, my trousers, and my shoes. So caustic was the stronger stuff that I jumped, fully clothed, into the shower to dilute it. It burnt my arm badly, I still have the scars!

"Why waste money on a plumber?" my mind repeated for the third time. "I'm a strong, intelligent male, I can do it." And I started making plans to have another try. I would wear sunglasses for protection in case the next reaction went anywhere near my eyes. I would put the ruined clothes back on, so I wouldn't ruin yet more. I would...

Then I came to my senses, thank goodness! Instead of believing my thoughts, I decided to call a plumber. He came the next day, and his call-out fee was just $50.

How much had the idea to believe my thoughts and do it myself cost me? The first trip cost maybe $5 plus car costs and my time. The second cost me perhaps

$10, more car costs and more time. The ruined clothes, some old, some new. Shirt, say $50. Trousers perhaps $100. Brand-new shoes, maybe a month old, $200. Between $300 and $400 in total. How much did the plumber cost? Less than a hundred.

So the net loss for believing my mind, and deciding to try and do it myself was in the neighborhood of $300. Plus the inconvenience of the blocked sink for four days, as well as the agony of serious burns on my arm!

. - - - - - - . - - - - - .

Is this thought true? Or untrue?

The mind presents us with thoughts on an ongoing basis. Yet how often do we automatically believe what it tells us, rather than questioning its thoughts?

A serious dilemma is that the mind sometimes does tell the truth. And yet, when hijacked by the self-sabotage mechanism (ssm), it does not! Most of the time, we can't quantify the cost of believing its untruths. Yet here I was able to count the financial loss, and I still have the scars to remind me of my folly!

Holidays can be the perfect exercise in unwrapping the mind's untruths, and unbuckling your belt. You're at a buffet, or a large family dinner. You've polished off one, maybe even two plates of food and yet it's so delicious, you decide you have room for a little more. You get some more, and when you're done, you are either comfortably satisfied, or you walk out feeling like a stuffed turkey on Thanksgiving Day. If you felt comfortable, your thoughts told you the truth. If you felt like the turkey, your ssm hijacked your thoughts; and yes, you actually acted like one.

Who decides whether or not to think a thought? If there's no clarity here then consider: Before we have made a decision to go to the store, do we allow our body just to jump in the car and start driving? This sounds ridiculous, doesn't it? Does our body decide to go somewhere and we just follow along? Or do we first decide, and then the body does our bidding?

If the answer to this vital question is still unclear, how about going to raid the kitchen for a midnight snack? Do we or our bodies make this decision? I'm a couple of pounds overweight, okay, okay, several pounds. This unease about my weight is a good indication of what happens here. Since the results are not entirely desirable, I can tell the ssm has been involved, I sometimes allow it to decide for me.

When you allow the ssm to decide what you think, you give power to the ssm. When you choose, then your energy goes to make you stronger. Your choice decides which becomes more powerful.

Regular, random, everyday thoughts come from the ssm, designed to distract us from what is really going on. To avoid change and prevent our progress. To bring us undesirable consequences. To help us stay where we are.

Thinking something through may be hard work at first, but the way to exceptional achievements is by investing the necessary effort yourself. You can't delegate any of the consequences, so don't delegate any of your thinking! Don't be gullible.

Just as the experts say, it's crucial to investigate what the mind says. Ask yourself which thoughts the mind comes up with are true, and which ones are not. Does it fit in with what you already know to be true? Does it make sense? Is it actually credible? Don't just believe the thoughts the mind gives you - investigate its story. As Katie Byron says:

> "There is only one problem, ever: your uninvestigated story in the moment.'

Questions 3.1

1   Do your thoughts always tell you the truth?

2   When do your thoughts not tell you the truth?

3   How do you ascertain if a thought is true or not?

4   Who decides whether or not you think a thought?

5   If your last answer was, 'Me, I do!' then what makes you think that? Can you choose not to think a thought?

• - - - - - - • - - - - - •

Yes, but what's the next step?

If you see anything here in this koan that looks familiar, or speaks to your heart, it suggests your self-sabotage mechanism may mislead you in this manner. What can you do about it? There are many possibilities, but one effective strategy which has stood the test of time is to address the root of the problem.

Any time that your mind gives you a thought, ask yourself whether it could be valid, or if it's maybe not true. Will it produce the long-term result you're looking for? Investigate each one. Especially those that seem questionable!

. - - - - - - - . - - - - - - - . - - - - - - . - - - - - .

3.2 If it's simple, it must be easy, right?

It tasted awful. I turned green, puked up my dinner, and my parents wondered why I was ill. But I couldn't tell them. I was a teenager and my parents had forbidden me to smoke, if I had told them I would have been grounded for a long, long time. But all the "cool kids" smoked, and back then I badly wanted to be cool.

Then one of them asked, "Why listen to your parents?" This seemed like such a good question, my parents knew so little when I was a teenager! So I had my first cigarette.

My desire to be cool fueled my determination to smoke. They say that perseverance is paramount, right? So I continued, a glutton for punishment. Some time later, I had reached my goal and could endure the discomfort, the awful taste, and the physical illness that inevitably followed. I had become a smoker, and thought myself a "cool kid." I was a success.

Lots later, as an adult, I finally realized that my parents were right. Smoking is indeed bad for you and can damage your health. So I decided to stop smoking.

In fact I've stopped smoking a dozen times, I'm a real expert. It wasn't that the first few days were not successful, it was that a month or two later, I kept going back to smoking again.

I knew that only one of my thirty cigarettes each day tasted good but, ahhh, that one... And my craving for the one that tasted heavenly was why I endured the other twenty-nine. No, I didn't see it quite this way at the time.

What strategies did I try? Let's see...

Willpower was the obvious choice: I just won't smoke. I was successful to start with, yet a few weeks later, I was back on cigarettes. Guess my will-power wasn't as strong as I thought it was.

Cutting down seemed another obvious possibility. I know! I told myself in a moment of monumental clarity: I'll gradually reduce until I'm at zero. This strategy had worked to cut down on the sugar I take in coffee, maybe it would work for smoking. What a laugh! This worked for maybe a week, and that's being generous.

I still hadn't figured out that I was actually addicted, so I kept on changing my behavior, totally ignoring the fact that the problem was me, rather than my strategy. After all, isn't blaming something else for our problems of the utmost importance? How can we feel all warm and fuzzy inside if we blame ourselves?

Still focused on what I was doing rather than my context, I thought up another change that seemed guaranteed to work this time: I know, I'll only smoke when I have a drink in my hand. That just got me to the bar at lunch time and immediately after work. The alcohol didn't do my job performance much good either.

How about: I'll only smoke after six at night? But then I spent most of the day fantasizing about how good that first cigarette would taste, and my work suffered almost as much.

Ah, thought I, the perfect solution: I'll only smoke when someone offers me a cigarette. So I begged and pleaded with my friends - and even people I didn't know - to offer me a cigarette. You can imagine just how popular I became!

Perhaps I'll wait until an opportune moment, which should help me stop for good. And so the next time my throat was so sore that each cigarette actually hurt, I stopped. A few weeks later, when my sore throat was completely better, I took another cigarette at a party. Surprise, surprise, that's all it took, I was hooked again.

It didn't take that long to realize that I was not strong-willed enough just to have the odd cigarette when I was at a party. Yes, that strategy was also one that I tried.

Jean-Pierre, my French friend, liked strong French cigarettes, and so I learned to smoke Gaulois as he did. The nicotine on my fingers built up and eventually became physically painful. I knew smoking was poisoning my body, but I was an addict. So I bought a cigarette holder, which alleviated the external symptoms. And I just ignored the internal ones. "Out of sight, out of mind" seemed like the right slogan to live by.

Ignoring the obvious

As I write this now, I am amazed at my ability to ignore the obvious. Was there a link between the frequent sore throats that I used to suffer from, and the rapidity with which they cleared up when I stopped? Oh, no, could my smoking have really been the cause of my sore throats. Was my suffering really self inflicted?

After numerous such failed attempts, I finally stopped trying to stop smoking. I realized that energy into the negative, stopping smoking, was still putting energy into smoking. I stopped putting energy into what had proved not to work and instead I decided to do what does.

I made good health now and long life in the future my ongoing choice. Then I was able to follow this oh-so-simple strategy to stop smoking. This strategy is permanent, immediately effective, and has never, ever failed. In fact, it's infallible.

Can it really be that simple? Yes. It is extremely simple to stop smoking. Just do this one thing. Never, ever, ever put another cigarette in your mouth. Ever.

If you do this, or rather don't do this one thing, then you've stopped smoking. Forever.

What could be simpler? Merely avoid this one action, never do this and you've stopped smoking for good. Yet as I, along with millions of others know from experience, simple does not mean easy.

● - - - - - - - ● - - - - - - ●

Simple and Easy

Simple things are simple. Quitting smoking is just a matter of never, ever putting another cigarette in your mouth.

Getting fitter is simple. Just do more than a half hour's cardiovascular exercise three times a week.

Becoming wealthy is simple. Always spend less than you earn.

Think about this, the reason why there's room for you at your local gym is because the large majority of people who join do NOT go frequently. They confuse the easy - signing up for the gym - with the simple - getting fit. A gym membership does not make us fit. It may be a step in the right direction, but to get fit, you need to work out regularly. Without this common misunderstanding, many health clubs would go out of business.

So, contrary to popular opinion, "simple" does not mean "easy", the two are NOT the same. In fact, there's just no correlation between the two. Simple can be difficult, and simple can be easy.

Sometimes the simple can be extremely difficult.

Questions 3.2

1   *What's the common misunderstanding about simple and easy?*

2   *How does the story about quitting smoking affect your understanding of simple and easy?*

3   *Why are gym memberships affordable, relatively speaking?*

4   *What strategy does work to stop smoking?*

5   *Why does choosing to do something rather than having to do it make a difference?*

. - - - - - - - . - - - - - - .

Yes, but what's the next step?

If you see anything here in this koan that looks familiar, or speaks to your heart, it suggests your self-sabotage mechanism may mislead you in this manner. What can you do about it? There are many possibilities, but one effective strategy which has stood the test of time is to address the root of the problem.

Wherever, whenever you see or hear the word simple, mentally add, "And simple does NOT mean easy!"

Only put your energy into what you do want, such as good health, rather than what you don't want - smoking. Phrasing it in the negative just doesn't work!

. - - - - - - . - - - - - - - - . - - - - - - . - - - - - .

3.3   Success Not Found in Common Hours

For three weeks in July 2005, I was at the gym virtually every day. Enjoying Lance Armstrong win his seventh Tour de France. My right knee was hurting, and it was all Lance's fault! (*smile* just kidding.)

As I sat on a stationary bike, I'd watch live TV with him on a real bike. My right knee had already been seriously damaged when I ran a marathon after my second cartilage operation. Yet seeing my cycling hero just tempted me to work harder. Why would I care about the consequences, the future, when it felt so right, right then?

It was enthralling!, Lance was on his way to winning his seventh consecutive

Tour de France, the world's premier professional cycle race. Faith along with belief in his abilities had got him his initial wins. Now he'd won so many times that he and I, along with most of the others involved, just knew he was going to win again.

Lance Armstrong is the only person to have won seven times, having broken the previous record of five consecutive wins by Spaniard Miguel Indurain. Yet back in 1996, Lance had dropped out of the Tour with testicular cancer, and his treatments included brain and testicular surgery and extensive chemotherapy. The prognosis was originally very poor. I recall reading that his doctor gave his chances of surviving as around ten percent!

In this, his last consecutive Tour de France, 2005, Lance won just the second individual time trial. Yet knowing how to play and win this game of chess on wheels, he won the Tour by the considerable margin of four minutes and forty seconds over second placed Ivan Basso.

Having won the Tour the six previous years, he had given himself the winning experience many, many times. He'd put in the serious effort it takes; the time, energy, and commitment to win enough races, and enough stages, to know he could do it. It wasn't just that he knew about winning, he had had so many authentic experiences! He really knew he could and would win the Tour de France. One time he even had an accident - he was pulled of his bike by a spectator - yet he still won.

He just let go! He knew he would win, so he had stopped worrying about winning. And the result showed in his domination of the race. He took the yellow jersey on the fourth day and, apart from relinquishing for just one day, the tenth, he held it all the way to the end. What a man. What mastery. What a hero!

· - - - - - · - - - - - ·

Authentic knowing vs knowing about

There's an enormous difference between just knowing about something and authentic knowing.

- Knowing about something just means we have received information from somebody else. We understand it, and can regurgitate it.

- Real knowing is authentic. This takes a lot more than just understanding - it takes experience. Just like exercise, you can't delegate it!

Experience is personal - an inside job. You know it's an inside job because you can't delegate it. You have to put in the work yourself - invest your own time and energy - to gain the experience.

People may think that believing, or having faith, is sufficient. Yet the theoretical knowledge of a brand-new MBA graduate, or a university professor, is rather different to empirical knowledge. A man may believe he understands childbirth, but only a woman can really know.

If someone does something when appropriate, they know it. If they do not do it when appropriate, they do NOT know it - although they may know about it.

We have all heard people say, for example, "I know I should stop smoking" when they instead mean, "I know about stopping smoking." If they really did know, they would have stopped smoking!

A key difference between understanding and knowing something is the amount of energy that we have put into it. "It" can be anything at all - such as winning the Tour de France, stopping smoking, or one of these koans.

Initial failure is normal

Failure is just part of the process. The word FAIL is wonderful, it's said to be an acronym which stands for "First Attempts in Learning."

Finding out what doesn't work is part of the learning process, being wrong is just a mistake. We all do it, we're all human, and it's indeed human to err. When we've discarded enough ways of what doesn't work, we're left with what does! So it can be critical, as well as very informative, to be wrong.

When we know that to move from understanding to real knowing takes time, energy, and experience, we are aware that energy is just what's needed.

Then expending the energy is not such a big effort, it's required. Which actually makes it easier to invest the necessary time and energy. There are lots of ways of putting in time and energy. Practicing, doing it, exercising, failing, making mistakes, repeating, applying, experiencing, studying, learning...

When we know that real knowing takes energy and experience, this enables us to become more effective at anything - anything at which we want more, better results. When we really know we just do it as and when appropriate.

This koan explains why so many consultants put in major effort, and then find that there's no lasting benefit from their efforts. Why so many teachers are often unsuccessful in the long-term. Why so many students fail at their endeavors. Success is indeed not found in common hours!

Questions 3.3

1   *What is the difference between real knowing and just knowing about something?*

2   *Who is the only one who can give you an experience?*

3   *How do you know if you really know?*

4   *Why is failure valuable?*

5   *What other benefits come when you know that time and energy is essential for authentic knowing?*

· - - - - - · - - - - - ·

Yes, but what's the next step?

If you see anything here in this koan that looks familiar, or speaks to your heart, it suggests your self-sabotage mechanism may mislead you in this manner. What can you do about it? There are many possibilities, but one effective strategy which has stood the test of time is to address the root of the problem.

Ensure you do take the actions suggested, which means putting in the effort to contemplate and then write down your answers to all the questions posed in the various chapters here. Don't believe or assume that knowing about self-sabotage is the same as real knowing. It isn't!

· - - - - - · - - - - - · - - - - - · - - - - - ·

3.4   Is there really a Most Important Question?

Henry looked drawn and a lot thinner, not at all well as he sat at the security desk. I hadn't seen him for months, nor was he his usual jovial self.

"What's up?" I asked. Henry was the superintendent in our apartment building, unless I needed something, we only saw each other occasionally.

"I had a heart attack, a double by-pass," he responded, and for the next five minutes I heard all the gruesome details. He was now on a serious diet, had lost maybe thirty pounds, and had another thirty to go. He'd stopped smoking - cold turkey - which I knew from previous conversations that he'd wanted to do for ages.

And he now allowed himself just one beer a week, rather than the half dozen a day that he'd been used to.

Henry had known that he had been seriously overweight, with a rather unhealthy lifestyle, yet had just ignored it. He'd told himself that he was invincible and it wouldn't happen to him, after all, he was only in his early forties, and only old people had heart attacks. Yet happen it did!

The doctor was blunt, even severe, "You'll be dead within ten years if you keep mistreating your body like this. You need to stop smoking, cut out alcohol and lose weight. And you need to start now, right now! Otherwise the next heart attack could kill you. Or you may not be so lucky, and instead end up severely incapacitated, hobbling about with a stick."

He'd known about wanting the results, and now he had the motivation...

. - - - - - - . - - - - - .

The crucial questions to ask

Most of us haven't yet figured out that there's an important question we need to ask ourselves.

This important question is, "Which of these four questions is the most important to me?'

1   Do I feel like doing it?

2   Do I want to do it?

3   Is it me? or

4   Do I want the results that doing it will bring?

We haven't said what "it" is, so this question is in the general rather than the specific.

No one answer is more right or wrong than another, it's just our answer, and we can't make a mistake, phew! Our answer is what's true for us. Although we need to remember that different answers have different consequences.

Yet this crucial question is one of the most influential we'll ever contemplate. Because the answer determines where we end up. It determines the circumstances of our life. Just as Henry found out here.

Before his heart attack, Henry had been telling himself that the first two, "Do I feel like smoking?" or "Do I want to have a beer?" were his most important questions.

How do we know this? His actions answered for him. As my mother used to say, "Actions speak louder than words." Wise woman, my mother!

Afterward, the second question, "Do I feel like doing it?" became irrelevant. So had the first! He changed his response to the fourth,"Do I want the results that living in a healthy manner will bring?"

We all need to put some serious time and energy into contemplating our answer here - Which of these four questions is the most important for me? Not anyone else, for me. We need forethought, to deliberate on our default answer, the automatic one that we come up with in general. As we change, we may find that our answer here also changes. Then we can give the most appropriate answer in each circumstance in particular.

Some people find that writing down the thoughts which come up while thinking seriously about their default general answer to be extremely helpful.

Questions 3.4

1   *What is your Most Important Question? When do you ask it?*

2   *Why is it essential to determine your Most Important Question?*

3   *Can you change your Most Important Question having once set it in general?*

4   *What are the results of choosing each option as your Most Important Question?*

5   *How does determining your general Most Important Question help you?*

• - - - - - • - - - - - •

Yes, but what's the next step?

If you see anything here in this koan that looks familiar, or speaks to your heart, it suggests your self-sabotage mechanism may mislead you in this manner. What can you do about it? There are many possibilities, but one effective strategy which has stood the test of time is to address the root of the problem.

Reflect on your Most Important Question. Contemplate, ponder this deeply.

Decide for yourself which really is the most significant for you. Realize all actions have consequences, and some consequences are more desirable than others. And others are more arduous!

• - - - - - • - - - - - - - - - • - - - - - - • - - - - - •

3.5   A really novel idea - Doing What Works!

In the ancient Greek classics, Sisyphus was a deceitful king who encouraged commerce, and then preyed upon travelers and guests. He had lots of run-ins with the Gods believing, even though he was a mere mortal, that he was cleverer than Zeus, the King of the Gods.

As punishment for his many crimes, Sisyphus was condemned to roll a boulder to the summit of a steep hill. However, before reaching the top, the huge stone would always roll back down again, thus forcing him to repeat the pointless task for eternity.

One empowering interpretation of this Sisyphean task, this thankless and endless endeavor, is that so long as Sisyphus saw it as a frustrating yet eternal activity he was condemned to repeat it. But when he changed his thoughts about the task, and instead chose to roll the boulder up the hill, this broke the curse and then he reached the top. The energy released by his let-go made the job less arduous. His change in context enabled him to complete the task and thus he set himself free.

• - - - - - - • - - - - - •

The infallible strategy for success

Here's what to do to achieve success; how to get you, indeed anybody, to where you desire to be. Just choose to:

1   Do what works for you to achieve whatever you seek to be, do, or have.

2   Do NOT do what doesn't work to get you there.

It sounds so simple and yes, you're right, it is indeed simple. So simple. Yet how many of us follow this simple advice?

Part of the problem is that we confuse simple and easy, see If It's Simple, It

Must Be Easy, earlier in this chapter. Simple does not mean easy, nor does it mean difficult. Some simple things are easy, and some of the simplest are very difficult. There's no correlation.

However, whether simple is easy or difficult, we need to do what does work for us, rather than what doesn't. If we choose to do more of what works to bring us long-term success say, then we'll be more successful. Simple! Yet as with most things saying it's simple - and it is simple - is not to say anything about how easy, or how hard, it may be!

How do we know if it works and what does not? Well, that's the simplest thing of all! If we're getting our desired results, then we're doing what works. If we're not getting what we want although we've persevered, we're probably not.

Simply put, what does not work is what we know will not get us there. If what we're doing is not working, then choose to do it differently, to do it some other way, or to do something else! Yet often the problem lies internally, in our context, in some uninvestigated thought which needs addressing first.

And when we continue doing what we know doesn't work for us, we're less successful. Unless you're willing to admit to being a masochist, you'll probably agree that this is undesirable. Isn't Benjamin Franklin's definition of insanity wonderful?

"To keep doing the same thing - while expecting a different result."

How many of us continue to repeat the same old things that make us miserable. Then we ignore the link between our choices and their consequences, and complain how unhappy we are. This suggests confusion, we don't know what we really want.

Sit back and reflect - What do you really want?

Listen to your inner self. Your gut, your vibe, your inner voice will take you toward your long-term desire. If you pay attention, your heart is pretty reliable in telling you what doesn't work for you, and what does.

Questions 3.5

1   *What happens when you do what works?*

2   *What happens when you do what doesn't work?*

3   *How can you tell what does and doesn't work for you?*

4   *When you're doing what doesn't work for you, what do you do?*

• - - - - - • - - - - - •

Yes, but what's the next step?

If you see anything here in this koan that looks familiar, or speaks to your heart, it suggests your self-sabotage mechanism may mislead you in this manner. What can you do about it? There are many possibilities, but one effective strategy which has stood the test of time is to address the root of the problem.

Train yourself to ask yourself what outcome you want in the circumstances, and whether the suggested course of action will bring you that outcome. I.e., remember to ask yourself, what works for me? and, what doesn't work?

• - - - - - - • - - - - - - - • - - - - - - • - - - - - •

3.6   Real Personal Power - an unusual insight

At the Zen retreat, it was late afternoon, the sun was shining and it was a lovely day in the beautiful mountains of the Western Cape. Our next meeting was coming up soon, and I had the schedule in my pocket.

Mary was from the USA, and this was her first visit to Africa. She was running the meeting and wanted to make sure she would be there on time. "When's the next meeting, at 6 or 6.30 p.m.?" she asked.

"Yes," I answered helpfully. She looked blank.

"Yes," I repeated, "it's at 6 or 6.30." She continued looking blank, perhaps thinking I hadn't heard her question properly.

Smiling, I explained. The next meeting will happen when it happens, and what you really want to know is when everyone will be there so you can start. You don't actually want the answer to the far less useful question, "When is it scheduled for?"

We're in Africa, I continued. And Africa runs on African time. Here schedules are loose, an approximation rather than a firm commitment. So everyone will show up when they get there and you'll start when it seems right for you to start. This will no doubt be some time after six, and probably before six thirty.

Mary seemed rather perplexed. "How can an organization run on such loose terms?" she asked.

Yet the meeting happened. Everyone who wanted to be there was there, and nobody stressed about being right on time. Those who chose to miss some of it missed the part they missed. The rest got the whole of her wonderful insights. It was, in fact, perfect.

• - - - - - - • - - - - - - •

Clarity, Awareness, and Power

When Mary stopped stressing about being on time, she changed her idea of what was decisive - and enjoyed herself as a result.

We all want to get to where we want to be, wherever that is. Our interest in learning to better cope with the self-sabotage mechanism acknowledges that we are not there yet. So what will enable us to get there? Change! Only by changing something. Effective change is vital because,

"Unless you make a change in your life, nothing will change in your life."

The usual next questions are, "What do we change?" and "How do we change?" But this assumes that we can change, of course.

So what enables us to change? The requisite power - personal power - which includes motivation. If someone is powerless, they can't make changes! So enough power is vital. The more power we have to make changes, the more we can change ...

Our answer to the basic question, "What and how do we change?" is in two parts:

1   create an effective strategy to get where we want to be, and

2   become more effective in implementing that strategy.

So how do we create an effective strategy? And what do we do to become more effective?

The keyword here is effective, we need to become aware of the differences that make the difference. Until we are aware of what does make the difference, how can we become effective in creating what we want?

So awareness - becoming aware of what's relevant - is crucial. As you might expect, awareness suggests a topic, a subject of which we may have been previously unaware. Simple, right?

Our new awareness can then lead us to clarity. Lack of clarity suggests a subject about which we have already become aware, but may not be very clear. The general versus the specific is a very good example in logic, most of us are aware that there is a significant difference, but many people aren't clear on what that difference is.

So what gives us clarity? Learning what's critical, the differences that make the difference, the crucial distinctions. We become clearer by studying what gives us more power in any specific circumstance. These koans mostly contain a distinction which can give us more power in some particular area. The more clear we are, the more power we have, and the more effective we can be.

So these distinctions, the differences that make the difference, these new perspectives into which we are investing our time and energy have the happy outcome of giving us more power over our circumstances.

Questions 3.6

1   *What's required to get you to where you want to be?*

2   *Who benefits when you change?*

3   *Why is it essential for you to become more aware?*

4   *How does clarity come into it?*

5   *When are you more effective?*

● - - - - - - ● - - - - - ●

Yes, but what's the next step?

If you see anything here in this koan that looks familiar, or speaks to your heart, it suggests your self-sabotage mechanism may mislead you in this manner. What can you do about it? There are many possibilities, but one effective strategy which has stood the test of time is to address the root of the problem.

Instead of fighting change, embrace it all! Recognize that internal change leads to external change and precedes manifestation of the results you want. So appreciating the necessity of changing your context is the first step to making any enduring changes in your life.

● - - - - - ● - - - - - - - ● - - - - ●

4 THE LAW OF ATTRACTION - HOW THINGS WORK

4.0   The Law of Attraction - Summary

Many people seem to have difficulty in getting the Law of Attraction to work consistently for them. So these are its three different aspects, the major components to improve your understanding of what's simply known as the Law of Attraction.

As always, please feel free to ignore any section of this book and move on to the next story. Some people prefer to start at the bottom with an example. Others like a structured top down approach, with a coherent explanation first.

The first aspect of the Law of Attraction is that Energy Energizes. Whatever you put your energy into will increase, no matter what it is. It doesn't matter whether you're being positive or negative, it increases - energy is energy.

Then there's the Focus Principle. Focus your energy, invest your energy into what you do want, not what you don't. This is often totally ignored.

The Golden Rule is the third part. What you do to others will be done unto you. What goes around, comes around. Other people tend to act toward you in the same way that you act toward others, although your actions won't necessarily be reciprocated by the same people.

Let's summarize these three aspects to the Law of Attraction with an example we recommend, always telling it like it is, telling the truth:

1   The Energy Principle, part One. You energize being in accord with reality, you increase telling the truth.

2   The Focus Principle, part Two. You put your energy into what you do want - people telling the truth. This word "people" includes everyone else, as well as you.

3   The Golden Principle, part Three. When you tell the truth to others, this energizes you being told the truth by others. This increases telling the truth by everybody.

In all three aspects, this strategy increases the truthfulness of the world. Since you're more effective when you focus on reality rather than illusion, we encourage this. And you may also wish to explore the consequences of lying instead, to see what happens. So tell the truth - consistently.

• - - - - - - - • - - - - - - - • - - - - - - - • - - - - - - •

4.1   The Law of Attraction, part One - Energy Energizes

A previous client, Neil, called us. He was rather despondent. Having started his own business close to a year earlier, it was now failing. He wanted to meet again - what was he doing wrong?

Over coffee, he related the sorry story of exactly what he'd been doing. Ever since he'd started his own business at the beginning of the year, he had been worrying about the future. How long would his money last? What happened if his clients all moved away? He'd actually foreseen needing to let his secretary go in October, because he would no longer be able to afford her salary.

What had happened? He had run out of money, many of his clients had moved away, and he had just let his secretary go - in the exact same month that he'd envisioned, October - because he could no longer afford her. His misdirected energy had created the result he'd been dreaming about!

. - - - - - . - - - - - .

The Energy Principle

Thoughts both have energy and are energy. So do emotions, feelings, and actions! And energy is creative. In fact, all of our energy is creative, it all has some effect. Energy energizes!

As Dr. Deepak Chopra says:

> *"Attention energizes ... Whatever you put your attention on will grow stronger in your life. Whatever you take your attention away from will wither, disintegrate, and disappear."*

Energy energizes - the Law of Attraction, part One - tells us that we increase whatever we put our energy into. Practice is a common way that we put in energy. Self-fulfilling prophecies are expressions of this principle of attraction. All energy energizes anything and everything, which then naturally increases in our lives.

Debbie, our editor, became crystal clear here when we asked her what she was really good at. She loves crocheting, has practiced a lot, and is very good at it. Then we looked at running, an activity she is not good at, and she saw that she'd put no energy into it. Then we asked about her daughter, Cheyenne. Debbie replied that the more positive energy she puts into her relationship, the more positive it becomes.

Whenever we put in energy, we invoke the Law of Attraction - no matter whether our energy goes into positively or negatively. Yet most of us miss this crucial second aspect, that it works both ways. Neil found this out the hard way, as have many of us in a relationship. We'll explore the implications more closely in the next koan, the Focus Principle - the Law of Attraction, part Two. Here we're looking at part One.

Energy always energizes. It does so for Neil, and Debbie, and athletes, businesses, the advertising industry, our relationships, everyone... If we put energy into wishing to develop a particular quality, life will bring us situations in which we can develop that. Our energy attracts situations which can help us progress. Initially, we may judge such situations as negative. Ten years later, we often see benefits which may be totally unexpected.

For example, we may say, God give me patience, (and I want it now!) Then what happens? The universe brings us the perfect situation in which to practice patience. When we are running late for a meeting there's a slow truck holding us up on the road which we cannot overtake. What an outstanding opportunity to develop patience!

The universe is on your side, and so to encourage you to change, it may increase the pressure. Now the self sabotage mechanism can negatively interpret this encouragement to change, and instead report that "things are getting worse." But actually your attention is simply being drawn more emphatically to your next change, rather than things are getting worse. This change of context may alter its entire meaning for you...

The Law of Attraction, part One, helps us release negative emotions by again bringing us the same sort of situation, perhaps more emphatically. Even slower trucks! Our energy may bring us what we don't want, or what we're afraid of. It can make our negativity, fear, anger, rage, dislike, etc. grow larger, stronger. All opportunities to progress! We benefit by receiving whatever we need to choose differently, to let it go and move on.

This aspect is demonstrated by this pithy story. Neil chose to put energy into his business failing, and it failed. He had a perfect opportunity to respond positively, but chose not to do so. He may have had such opportunities previously, but instead reacted as before. He successfully created what he had visualized. The chances are good that another such possibility will come so he can choose differently and enjoy a more positive outcome.

When we're negative, and wish to stop enduring the inevitable consequences, our energy brings us situations that challenge us to improve. And our discomfort grows whenever we decline to change. This helps explain why an uncomfortable situation will come up again later. And why such circumstances often repeat themselves. Sisyphus, see Chapter Three, eventually got the point that the constant repetition of his situation was simply encouragement for him to change. And when he changed, so did the outcome.

We progress when we instead choose to respond positively - rather than react the same as last time. Why continue to do the same thing and continue to experience the same result? There's a good word for this - boring!

How can we avoid such situations? We do so when we stop reacting to what happens. When we see that impatience is not wrong, it just doesn't serve us. Nor does anger, or the frustration we feel when we react negatively to reality, to what's happening. We grow by changing our response.

We benefit when we instead choose our response mindfully. Conscious choosing, aka conscious living, comes from conscious thinking.

Create the feeling of having it, and be grateful for having it, and your positive energy will help you have it when the time is right. As the movie, The Secret, says,

"What we think about, and what we thank about, we bring about."

Questions 4.1

1   *Describe the Law of Attraction, part One.*

2   *What do many people miss here?*

3   *When does is it operate?*

4   *Who does this Law benefit?*

5   *How do we choose a strategy which works?*

● - - - - - - ● - - - - - - ●

Yes, but what's the next step?

If you see anything here in this koan that looks familiar, or speaks to your heart, it suggests your self-sabotage mechanism may mislead you in this manner. What can you do about it? There are many possibilities, but one effective strategy which has stood the test of time is to address the root of the problem.

Reflect that energy energizes. Contemplate this, check that it is your truth. If it is, then put energy into the results you wish to see in your life. All the results. Which suggests that work, making money is just one of many priorities in your life. Your relationship with your partner, and your kids, need energy. So does your relationship with yourself! Yet how many of us forget to give enough quality time to ourselves?

• - - - - - - • - - - - - - • - - - - - - • - - - - - •

4.2   The Focus Principle - the Law of Attraction part Two

She was lovely. Absolutely gorgeous.

Kate was a brand new friend; we'd had a marvelous exchange of ideas, of energy, of each other. Although we'd only met an hour or so before, we felt as though we'd known each other for ages. If she had been single, I would have been very interested, but it didn't matter that she was already involved, the energy between us was almost spiritual.

We should get together sometime, we agreed. Then she explained that she had dinner parties from time to time. "I'll invite you to the next one," smiled Kate. Then she saw my hesitation, my frown. "What's wrong?" she asked.

"Lots of people tell me that," I explained, "but they never do. I don't know why but it just never happens."

"I'm different, I keep my promises," she said. Yet I just knew that she wouldn't.

And she didn't. Months later, I was still waiting. She never did call. I never saw Kate again.

Yet is this story about the fickleness, the unreliability of women? Or is it a story about the importance of focusing on what we do want, rather than what we don't; along with the power of our mind to energize whatever we put our energy into.

• - - - - - • - - - - • - - - •

The Focus Principle

The Focus Principle - the Law of Attraction, part Two - tells us how to apply the first aspect, Energy Energizes. It tells us to focus on what we do want, rather than what we don't want.

Mother Teresa understood this principle perfectly. She replied, "Attend a march against war? No thank-you!" She was definitely not interested. But she went on to add, "But if you have a march for peace, then invite me. I'll be there!" Such brilliant clarity!

The advertising industry well understands both these parts of the Law of Attraction. Smoking increased significantly when smoking by the major star in films became the norm rather than the exception, role models fulfill their role when advertising.

TV adverts work by putting a few seconds' energy into behaviors they want us to copy. The TV industry tell their advertisers that adverts do work, yet they deny any connection between the increased violence in the world, and the increased violence in the programs which last a lot longer than a few seconds. Is it any wonder the older generation spend their time longing for the days of The Waltons and I Love Lucy?

We sabotage ourselves whenever we put energy into what we don't want. Rather put energy into our desires, into what we do want. Examine our thoughts, all of them, think the thoughts that serve us, and let the others go. Why continue a path to its inevitable dead end? Have you ever heard the term beating your head against a brick wall? It's uncomfortable. Trust me, I've tried it!

What happens when we tell ourselves:

- "I always lose my keys." or,

- "I can never remember names!" or,

- "I don't have the time!" or,

- *"I can't afford it!"*

The Focus Principle tells us that such thoughts energize what we don't want! And therefore what we don't want increases! Rather pay positive attention to what we do want to happen, since the way we pay attention creates the experience that ensues.

Instead say, "I'm getting better at looking after my keys." Then put them where you'll look next time. Maintain, "I am getting better at remembering names," and then put energy into remembering someone's name. Rather ask, "How can I find the time, or the money?" This puts energy into it being possible and then you can make a plan.

Remember that all actions have consequences. So focus on whatever you seek to be, do, or have. Attract only what you do want. Rather avoid the headaches that brick walls bring.

Most of us do what we think is right at the time. But this doesn't always give us the result that we want, as I can attest to - and likely so can you. Look instead at how to think more effectively. Explore changing any and all ineffective beliefs - even though we may think they are right - to ones more productive in achieving what we want.

There's that wonderful apocryphal story about Nazruddin searching under the street lamp for his keys. After searching fruitlessly for a while, one of his students asked where had he lost them? "Over there," he replied, pointing away from the street lamp. "Then why are we looking here?" the student replied. "There's light here, searching is so much easier!"

Rather be totally unconcerned at how easy, or how difficult, you perceive changing your ineffective beliefs to be...

Questions 4.2

1   *What is the Focus Principle?*

2   *How can you tell that Mother Teresa really understood this Principle?*

3   *Why is this distinction so crucial? Reflect on its impact in society.*

4   *When do we use this Principle to sabotage ourselves?*

5   *Who might find this Principle difficult to apply?*

. - - - - - - . - - - - - .

Yes, but what's the next step?

If you see anything here in this koan that looks familiar, or speaks to your heart, it suggests your self-sabotage mechanism may mislead you in this manner. What can you do about it? There are many possibilities, but one effective strategy which has stood the test of time is to address the root of the problem.

Ensure you only put energy into what you do want, rather than what you don't! Which suggests that you need a clear idea of your real priorities in life. Ask yourself, what will be significant at the end of my life? How many of us will answer, I wish I had spent more time at the office, working...

. - - - - - . - - - - - . - - - - - . - - - - .

4.3   The Golden Rule - the Law of Attraction part Three

"He does a lousy job and I don't know why people come here," said the old man. I was startled, he was a complete stranger and it seemed a rather peculiar way to start a conversation, even if he was a dissatisfied customer.

"Really," said I in Len's defense, "I've invariably found him very reliable, he does an excellent job servicing my car, and his prices are reasonable. He's also courteous and willing."

"Hmm," grunted the old man, "I've known him longer than you." And that conversation with a stranger in the mechanic's garage was over.

Later I asked Len what the old man's problem was. "I really appreciate that," he laughed as he thanked me for coming to his defense. "He's my father, and that's just his way of telling me that he loves me!"

A couple of years later, late on a Friday afternoon, my clutch started giving problems. So I called Len to tell him about my woes. "Can you drive it?" he asked. "Yes, but only in first gear," I replied. "Then drive it down here and I'll have a look."

It must have been nearly closing time when I got there. "Yes," he confirmed, "it's the clutch. If I rush, I can get to the parts department before they close."

I thanked him in reply and went for a cup of coffee in the café around the corner. Then my phone rang, "It's a bit more than the price I quoted," said Len, "Do you want it?" "What are my alternatives?" I wondered. "You've only got one - wait until Monday and I'll see if I can source a cheaper one."

But then I would have no car for the weekend, I noted - I was definitely willing to pay the higher price!

So Len purchased the clutch, installed it there and then, and at seven p.m. on Friday night, well after the regular five p.m. closing time, my car was back on the road.

I imagine that Len would have done this for any one of his customers, but it certainly did no harm that I'd defended him to an apparently dissatisfied customer - his father!

· - - - - - · - - - - - ·

The Golden Principle

My mother used to preach the third part of the Law of Attraction, the Golden Rule. "Do unto others as you would have them do unto you." I didn't understand what this meant while I was growing up, and I certainly didn't let anyone off the hook when I perceived that they had hurt me!

For me, revenge was sweet, and I didn't see the damage that such thoughts helped create. I ignored my bad feelings and blamed them for the way I was feeling. It was their fault! At that time I had never heard of the Law of Attraction, and I certainly didn't understand that energy energizes.

Now we've all heard, "What goes around, comes around." "As you sow, so shall you reap." The Bible puts it as: "So in everything, do to others what you would have them do to you." Or, if you're scientifically inclined, Newton's Third Law of Motion is: "Action and reaction are equal and opposite." These all express this third aspect to the Law of Attraction in different ways.

What we put into life, life gives back to us is one of the Laws of the Universe. The Golden Rule is one of the ways in which our inner state is reflected in our outer environment. The universe reverses all imbalances in the long run. Whether it's negative or positive, to give is indeed to receive.

This implies that what we do to other people will come back to us. Sooner or later, someone else will act the same way to us. "Those who live by the sword, die by the sword!' Anything somebody does to us could be this principle reflecting our previous actions back at us. We just don't know. We may be on the receiving end of the Golden Rule because of OUR past, perhaps unremembered, actions!

This suggests that it makes absolute sense for us all to follow the Golden Rule. If you don't want to be mistreated, do not mistreat others. If you find it unpleasant to receive negative actions, do not treat other people negatively. Only do unto others as you like being done to you!

Questions 4.3

1   *What is the third part of the Law of Attraction?*

2   *Why is this fundamental?*

3   *Who does this rule affect?*

4   *What are the implications of the Golden Rule?*

• - - - - - • - - - - •

Yes, but what's the next step?

If you see anything here in this koan that looks familiar, or speaks to your heart, it suggests your self-sabotage mechanism may mislead you in this manner. What can you do about it? There are many possibilities, but one effective strategy which has stood the test of time is to address the root of the problem.

Before you do anything for or to anyone else, ask yourself if you'd like someone else to do this to you? If not, then don't do it!

• - - - - - - • - - - - - - • - - - - - - • - - - - - - •

4.4   A rather Different View of How Life Works

Waa, I cried, Waaa. At six years old, the slap hurt! Life was serious. I kept on crying.

My mother had had enough, I had been disturbing the peace for far too long and she was exasperated. "Stop crying," she said. I ignored her, I was far too bound up in how bad it felt.

"Stop crying," she repeated loudly! But I continued wailing, it hurt too much. "If you don't stop crying, I'll make you stop!" she warned.

She was telling me to develop self-control, and at that tender age I had little or none. So I continued crying. And she smacked me again. Waaaa, I wailed. Another smack, and Waaaaa, I cried some more. This continued for what seemed like forever, although realistically it was probably only several minutes. Eventually, I realized that she wasn't going to stop, and so I had to. And did.

I never cried again as a boy, in fact it took many, many years before I was able to cry again over anything. Now, when things really move me, I do cry for happiness, for joy, but rarely for pain, sadness or sorrow.

Women sometimes say they want a sensitive man, in touch with his feelings. Yet I know why most of us don't cry - our mothers beat it out of us when we were kids!

For years I thought my mother was a witch, evil, and I had little respect for her.

It also took me many, many years to see that she had what I can now construe as a valid viewpoint. Who better to teach me to stop crying than my mother who loved me? Which would cause me less pain in the long term? To learn the lesson when young, or wait until someone way less caring taught me the same lesson in a far more brutal fashion?

Yet there's an even greater benefit that I only recently realized. "I'm OK, You're OK!" is a book on psychological interactions that I read years ago. Apparently when growing up, most of us chose the I'm Not OK position when our parents tell us they're right - and we're wrong - as they discipline us. Yet this along with various other incidents had me decide at a very early age that I'm OK, and my mother was Not OK.

See the immense benefits! I learned to think for myself, to take responsibility for myself, and to investigate someone else's thinking when they tried to persuade me of something. If it isn't rational, if it makes no sense, then I reject nonsense as nonsense. In fact, even when it sounds plausible, I still like to check it out for myself.

● - - - - - - - ● - - - - - ●

The Circle of Life

You are responsible for the circumstances of your life. Totally responsible!

This doesn't mean that other people and situations haven't had some influence, small or large, but only you are totally responsible for your part in creating your circumstances. This is good news! In fact, it's outstanding news! Why?

Actions have consequences. All actions have consequences, including all your actions! Some actions you can influence, some you can't. Actions which impact your life have consequences for your life. Your actions, which are all in the past, have had consequences. The sum total of all the consequences in your life amount to your circumstances.

To make changes in our life, it makes sense to focus on those aspects which we can affect. These are our actions, our thoughts, our beliefs. And we are totally responsible for what we think, and what we believe!

Being negative about our present circumstances doesn't change them. It's just not effective. While being positive today allows us to do something about tomorrow's circumstances. We can affect our circumstances in a positive manner by changing our actions which means changing our thinking which involves changing our beliefs.

This is only possible when we take responsibility for our situation. Total responsibility for ourselves and our circumstances. We are totally responsible anyway, but without acknowledging this fact, we don't have the power that taking responsibility brings! And then we feel powerless, and complain about the circumstances! Rather use the feedback given by the current circumstances to change our beliefs.

Changing our beliefs can sometimes be viewed as scary. But where do our beliefs come from: our parents, upbringing, society, school, family, friends, teachers, environment? As children we tend to accept without question, so beliefs are usually accepted without critical examination. Rarely does anyone choose their beliefs on the basis of whether they produce desirable results. Or even ask if they make any sense.

How believing gives your power away

Many people give their power away by believing others, sometimes no matter what they say. Yet without checking, how can you know the accuracy of any particular perspective? They may have a hidden agenda.

Or you disagree as an emotional reaction, regardless of how much sense they are making. You can be easily manipulated, either by others, or by your self-sabotage mechanism, when you don't take full responsibility for your beliefs, your context, and your actions.

We don't believe in believing, we believe in knowing instead. Authentic knowing gives real results. So if we're not getting the results we desire, or have any confusion about things, it may be because we haven't investigated our beliefs. Our beliefs cause us to think the way we think, which result in our actions (or inactions), which result in our circumstances.

There's peace in knowing the truth and, just like exercise, you can't delegate arriving at the truth. It may be the other person's truth, or even a reliable fact, but without investigation how can it be your truth? Without taking responsibility, without spending the time to check it out, any assertion can only be a belief.

Now some of the beliefs you have adopted will indeed be true. And yet some aren't! At best, other people don't have your best interests at the top of their priority list. They may have just adopted someone else's beliefs without any investigation. At worst, they may have a hidden agenda. This is why there's little peace in being gullible, in just believing the assertions of others. You can believe what they say, but you won't know for certain that anything is true without investigating it for yourself.

Questions 4.4

1   *What is the most compelling lesson my mother taught me?*

2   *Why is this so valuable?*

3   *Who is totally responsible for the circumstances of your life?
     Discuss your answer.*

4   *What is the drawback of believing others? Of believing any belief
     itself?*

• - - - - - - • - - - - - •

Yes, but what's the next step?

If you see anything here in this koan that looks familiar, or speaks to your heart, it suggests your self-sabotage mechanism may mislead you in this manner. What can you do about it? There are many possibilities, but one effective strategy which has stood the test of time is to address the root of the problem.

Formally take responsibility for your part in the circumstances which you find yourself, as well as for your entire life. Perhaps write such a statement down, sign and date it, then put it on your bathroom mirror. Recognize that you indeed played a part, and the part you played was essential in creating the whole. Taking full responsibility gives you the power to change your circumstances. Very empowering!

• - - - - - • - - - - - - - • - - - - - - • - - - - - •

4.5   How stressful can life be anyway?

My stress levels jumped through the roof. How on earth will I ever learn all this? I thought. There's no way anybody could!

My instructor had just started my first driving lesson. I was seated in his car, and he'd gone through the basics. "This is the steering wheel, and the first instruction is never to take your hands off the wheel, since this is how you steer the car."

"Yes Sir," said I.

"The road is in front of you, and to steer, to miss the other cars you need to keep your eyes on the road."

"Okay," I agreed.

Those are the two fundamental principles," he emphasized, "keep your eyes on the road and your hands on the wheel." He stopped for a breath. "These two are vital, absolutely vital! Never, ever forget them."

"Yes Sir," I repeated.

"Now, keeping those in mind, this is the gear lever, this is the hand-brake, this controls the lights while moving it that way controls the wipers, this is for the indicators, this..." He went on and on. Eventually he got to the radio. "You can forget about the radio for the moment," he said reassuringly.

Great! I thought, twenty things to remember at once, and now we're down to nineteen. I wasn't brimming with confidence; it seemed an awful lot to remember.

Then he pointed to my feet. "These three pedals work the accelerator, the brake and the clutch."

Three pedals, I'm not allowed to look, and I only have two feet! I panicked silently as my stress levels went through the roof.

However, I knew other people had learned to drive, and with patience and application, I knew I could too. This helped diminish my stress, and in due course, eventually, I passed my driving test.

One day, as I drove down the road, I realized that driving was no longer taking one hundred percent of my concentration. My stress levels were decreasing. I'm really getting the hang of this, I exulted. And so I decided to turn on the radio! Of course, since I was now an expert, I didn't need to stop. I took my hands off the wheel, and my eyes off the road, and nearly had my first accident. More stress!

Yet now, sometimes, I arrive home and think; where did the journey go? I don't remember driving home at all! I'd driven on auto-pilot, and come all the way without any stress at all.

● - - - - - - ● - - - - - - ●

The Stress Curve

The four stages in learning any new capability are:

a   Unconscious Incompetence

b   Conscious Incompetence

c   Conscious Competence

d   Unconscious Competence.

When we don't even know we don't know, there's no stress. As children in a car, we just knew it was moving. When very young, we had no awareness of driving and there's no stress when we're unconscious of our incompetence.

When we move to understanding that we don't know, stress starts building. Our stress can increase rapidly as we start to learn a new capability. When we really get that we don't know, that we're incompetent, the stress can become quite overwhelming.

As the new capability starts needing less than one hundred percent of our attention we become more competent and our stress starts to decreases.

We've become unconsciously competent when we arrive home and sometimes can't remember the journey. We are now great at driving, rather than just good. As a result, stress virtually disappears.

Stress can occur because we don't understand, or the mind thinks something is going to be difficult. Sometimes we stress because we don't like the feeling of not being in control. But real control, just like real understanding, isn't possible until we've been through the learning process. The gap between reality and what we think "should be" can be very stressful.

So stress seems to accompany most/all learning, all new capabilities. It seems to continue for quite a long while into the learning process itself. So accept that acquiring any new competence can involve stress, that's just the way things are.

When we realize this, then all the stress the mind creates is normal - just par for the course. Then we need not feel anxious about feeling stressed. Knowing this actually reduces the stress involved in most/all change. Since change is a constant in life, some stress is inevitable - so accept it.

In this introduction to self-sabotage, you're learning to change your beliefs, to change your thinking. Now most people find this a bit like asking out their first boy or girl. Yes, I know, it's not that exciting, but it can be just as nerve wracking. If you find any of our rather different perspectives causing you stress, just know It's entirely normal. So remember this insightful koan, as well as the earlier one, Is there really a Most Important Question, see Chapter Three.

In fact, life seems to test us when we declare ourselves as something. We say we want more patience and, rather than patience itself, life brings us situations in which we have to develop more patience. We say we want more money, and then we lose a source of income!

So our life can become more stressful as we decide to put effort into becoming more capable, more effective. Life doesn't give us strong muscles, it brings us situations in which we can develop strong muscles. And until our muscles are strong, a serious workout can be very stressful. Yet sooo very rewarding.

Questions 4.5

1.   *What is the mistaken but common view of stress illustrated in this koan?*

2.   *Who finds learning stressful?*

3.   *When does stress diminish?*

4.   *How else can you reduce stress?*

. - - - - - - . - - - - - - .

Yes, but what's the next step?

If you see anything here in this koan that looks familiar, or speaks to your heart, it suggests your self-sabotage mechanism may mislead you in this manner. What can you do about it? There are many possibilities, but one effective strategy which has stood the test of time is to address the root of the problem.

Contemplate the very first paragraph - "Life is difficult." - of Scott Peck's book, How I Found Freedom in an Unfree World. He then goes on to explain that knowing this is true makes life easier. Reflect when you know that change is stressful, then that knowledge makes stress easier to bear. This can actually reduce any stress!

. - - - - - - . - - - - - - - - . - - - - - - . - - - - - .

5 DON'T GIVE YOUR POWER AWAY!

5.1   Since I'm right, you must be wrong!

"How come your expense claim is so high?" complained Ian.

This seemed so very unfair! Ian ran the company, he was my boss, and he knew exactly why! I had completed the new system in some three months rather than the year it would have taken anyone else. He wasn't even paying for my overtime! But he was complaining about reimbursing my expenses.

Vicky, the love of my life, lived with Adrian, and yet started a clandestine relationship with me. It was fine to start with, but I soon missed being able to go to parties and out to restaurants as a couple. Although she continued to tell me how much she loved me, she didn't leave him. So I pushed her to break up with him.

One day I'd had enough of the secrecy and confronted both of them. From her lips, I was crushed to hear her say that she actually loved Adrian rather than me. And the reason why she had kept me hanging for so long? Life with me would be more comfortable. I had better prospects than Adrian, a truck driver!

I needed to recover from falling in love, or rather from the devastating effects of falling out of love. And hard work was the available antidote. So, day and night, I worked and slept. Basically, that was all. Three highly productive months later, the new system was finished. Yet to complete a computer system, you need computer time, and the nearest mainframe was forty miles away in another town. Hence the expense report.

Ian then had every entry on my expenses checked, and found just one day in the three months for which the computer log had no entry.

"Why did you claim expenses for that day?" he asked. Ah, I recalled, I did go there every day as I had said, but that day it wasn't to do any work. I'd forgotten I had attended a friend's wedding.

I was actually amazed that he was being so mean about such a small amount of money when I hadn't even attempted to claim overtime pay! Our perspectives were so very different; Ian was concerned about the monthly expenses vs. budget, while I was pleased at the effective and early completion of the whole project.

● - - - - - - ● - - - - - - ●

Being Right

Everyone is right from the limited perspective from which they come. So I'm right does not mean you are wrong, even when what we say may apparently be contradictory. When we're both looking at a piece of paper, you may see nothing on the side facing you, yet there may be a picture on the side facing me. We will disagree about the picture, because we have a different perspective.

Ian was right. The fact was that I had forgotten I hadn't worked one day. Yet I had also put in several hundred hours of overtime, which he did not offer to pay me for!

Being right is often not that significant - despite the inevitable disagreement of the ssm - and it can actually be irrelevant. Yet, how many of us like being right?

Along with mending my broken heart, the completion of the client's system, both ahead of schedule, and below budget, was the fundamental priority to me. The client totally agreed. So would have Ian, if he'd thought about the long-term health of the company!

To Ian, being right was key. And expenses had exceeded his monthly budget. Yet I hadn't tried to cheat on my expenses, I had made a mistake about one day in the past, one single fact. Instead of being congratulated for a job well done, I felt used and abused. Next time, I was certainly not going to work as hard. As company manager, his motivational methods left a lot to be desired!

Being right tells us nothing about being effective. Each viewpoint is simply as effective, or ineffective, as it is. And if we insist we are right, this can detract from any effort to become more effective. Being right can be seen as a disease!

To be more effective, we need to change our perspective. Without change, nothing will change. Without changing our attitude, it's difficult to become more effective. Yet agreeing that I'd made a mistake allowed me to resolve the situation and move on. And to decide that, rather than assume I knew, I'd check the facts next time. Ian didn't change and the long-term health of the company suffered.

The extra power to move on came from becoming clear about what had seemed wrong to start with - I didn't initially realize I'd made an error. Remember - I used to think I never made mistakes!

Note that this did NOT require a change by Ian. It only requires a change by one person. The other doesn't need to change.

This change in perspective can be used to resolve arguments. It's a decision we can make unilaterally, it only takes one. The other person can remain the same. Yet our willingness to explore their viewpoint may also make them more open-minded, although not in this situation. And if we get to truly appreciate their perspective, how can we say they are wrong - even if we see they have made a mistake?

A new perspective can change our beliefs which will change our thinking which changes our actions which changes our circumstances. It all starts, and ends, with us!

Questions 5.1

1   When you disagree with someone, and you are sure you are right, does that mean the other must be wrong?

2   What can you tell about a disagreement in which you being right does mean that the other person is indeed wrong?

3   How are being right and being effective connected? Discuss your answer.

4   What does this tell us about being right, and being effective?

5   How does this help us resolve an argument?

· - - - - - - · - - - - - ·

Yes, but what's the next step?

If you see anything here in this koan that looks familiar, or speaks to your heart, it suggests your self-sabotage mechanism may mislead you in this manner. What can you do about it? There are many possibilities, but one effective strategy which has stood the test of time is to address the root of the problem.

Whenever anybody disagrees with you, remind yourself this may simply mean that they must have a different perspective than you. Then find out what their viewpoint is and why they hold it...

· - - - - - · - - - - - - - - - · - - - - - ·

5.2   If you're ever in a bad mood...

"What shall I do?" implored the frantic voice on the phone. "I can't see a client in this state!" It was my good friend, Joan. And she needed help right then - this very instant!

Her boss had just been on her case. Yet again. As a result, she was in a very bad state mentally. Her mind was going round and round in circles: He had said this, which wasn't true, and missed out on the other, which was significant. This was unfair, and he'd said nothing about that... I knew exactly what she meant; my mind does the same sometimes.

Yet Joan is a real estate agent, and had an appointment with an influential prospect in an hour or so. How would she be able to focus on her client and his needs in this state? What should she do?

"What gives you pleasure?" I asked. No answer. "What makes you feel better when you're feeling down?"

There was a pause, then the first answer -"Dancing. I really enjoy dancing," said she in a small voice. "And..." I encouraged her to continue.

"Going for walks, long walks. Lovely music..."

"If you do what makes you feel good, even though your mind is racing and giving you no peace, then you'll feel better."

"I can't go dancing or for a walk right now," she objected. Her self-sabotage mechanism had hijacked her mind, and was now resisting any attempt to resolve the situation.

"Yet if you don't do something different, how is anything going to change?" I asked.

It was a big effort, but she put on some favorite music in the car, went somewhere she wouldn't be seen, and danced to it for a while. Then she continued playing the same tape as she drove to meet her client.

. - - - - - . - - - - - .

Bad mood strategies

Sometimes, for no apparent reason, you may find yourself just not very happy - or even trapped in a black mood. It can be useful to have some strategies to use if this ever happens. So create them in advance, when you're in a good mood. The more the merrier. Everyone around benefits when you know what to do to improve your emotional state - and you actually do it.

When you're feeling good about yourself, use some of that energy to come up with a dozen or more activities which can get you feeling better about yourself. Do this right now, since when you're down it's tough to be positive! Small things, not time consuming, that you can do when you are not entirely happy with your state.

You benefit by choosing strategies which don't require the presence of another person or a particular place. That place - anyone, or anything special - may not be around. Your partner may be the reason you're in a bad mood in the first place!

Some people find that knowing the reason that they're in a bad mood can help break it, so putting effort into discovering the reason can also be very rewarding.

Advance planning for when you need to improve your state can be very fruitful!

Questions 5.2

1   *What is the benefit of planning strategies in advance to improve your mood?*

2   *Who benefits if you do something enjoyable when you are in a black mood?*

3   *Why rely on strategies you can perform solo to improve your state?*

4   *Which specific strategies could help improve your mood next time you need a lift? Plan ahead now!*

● - - - - - - - ● - - - - - - ●

Yes, but what's the next step?

If you see anything here in this koan that looks familiar, or speaks to your heart, it suggests your self-sabotage mechanism may mislead you in this manner. What can you do about it? There are many possibilities, but one effective strategy which has stood the test of time is to address the root of the problem.

Plan ahead. Put some work into choosing some simple black mood strategies that work for you. Then decide to make yourself actually use them whenever you need to lift your state!

● - - - - - - - ● - - - - - - - ● - - - - - - ●

5.3   He Should - help or hindrance?

"It's been stolen!" I repeated incredulously, "Stolen?" I couldn't believe my ears!

I had lent my car to Lana, whom I barely knew, and now it was gone. I was upset. Very upset. Yet this was only the start of a long, sorry saga!

A friend had introduced me to Lana, who had some woeful story about her car. I was unclear on the details, but she needed a car, so would I lend her my spare one?

Sure, I said, seeing a chance to help a friend, and receive a little money to help pay for its expenses at the same time. Now it was time to pay me the nominal sum we had agreed upon. But her younger lover was taking her for a ride. Apparently she was besotted, she was paying all his expenses and they needed more money. As a potential source, my car was irresistible!

No one will know if we sell the car, and the owner will get the insurance money anyway, the boyfriend seems to have suggested. We get the money and nobody loses!

A crooked car dealer was very willing to cooperate. He changed the engine number along with the bumpers, put on different wheels with worn tires to change the way it looked, and sold my car! Lana then reported it to the police as stolen. And called me to tell me the same story.

But since the police had suspicions about the boyfriend, and the car dealer, they traced my car. "When can you come down and identify it?" they later called to ask.

When Lana knew the police had traced my stolen car, she called me. "I'm very, very sorry," she sobbed, "I don't want to go to prison, please don't press charges."

Just a few hours later, Lana's husband Bob called wanting to meet urgently to discuss the matter. So we met that same evening. "Please don't charge Lana with theft," he pleaded, "I'll pay for everything, all the repairs and charges and ensure you don't lose financially."

His categorical assurance reassured me. As far as I could tell, he was telling the truth at the time, and so I didn't bother to get this in writing. Big mistake!

Months later, when all the bills were in; the repairs for the damage, new tires, the towing charges, as well as the lawyer's time to legally get the car back on the road, it all totaled several thousand dollars.

Yet their lawyers offered me less than a thousand for the costs in total. So I called Bob and asked him what had he meant by ensuring I won't lose financially? Because now it was time to reimburse me, it seemed as though it was a rather different story...

Should he, or should he not keep his word, he wondered. "No one is telling me that I have to do that," he eventually reported.

Yet he knew that he didn't feel good about the situation. So he kept trying to find some way in which he could rationalize not reimbursing me as he had promised. "Why hadn't I insured it against theft?" he asked, ignoring the fact that my car hadn't been stolen. I had given the keys to Lana, and she then fraudulently sold it. The legal position turned out to be that it wasn't actually stolen, rather she had committed fraud!

Yet if I had made him wrong, told him he should reimburse me the full amount immediately as he had promised, the conversation would probably have ended immediately. The world is full of people who tell us we should do something we don't want to do and furthermore we should do it right now. Yet in general, how effective is such advice?

• - - - - - • - - - - - •

The Shoulds

Whenever we say or think they "should" do it, we are not giving them a choice. Usually we think they should have because, in fact, they haven't! So it's just our opinion and we're arguing with reality.

When we make someone else wrong, they usually know and will often make us wrong in return. In the I love Lucy show, whenever Ricky says "Lucy you got some 'splaining to do," Lucy inevitably comes up with some outlandish explanation and the angrier Ricky becomes the more outlandish Lucy's response gets.

Normally, what someone has done is because they saw it as the right thing to do. Yet we disagree, we know they should not have done it, we know better than them. We think they are wrong!

Our thinking that someone else is wrong causes us stress, internal conflict. And the self-sabotage mechanism has hijacked our thoughts yet again.

Yet when are we most effective? When we're stressed and mentally in pain? Or when we are happy and carefree? I'm choosing not to stress here, because I don't hold that he should reimburse me, although I agree it would be nice. I find I'm more effective when I don't need to waste energy coping with stress or pain. Then I have more for the task at hand.

Rather just accept what has happened as reality, and then use the opportunity to explore the validity of our thinking. How can we know for sure what someone else is aiming to achieve?

Much of the time, we find that what we hold as a must, or a should, is simply our preference, an opinion with few if any major long-term negative repercussions. Yet another area to let go of and simply enjoy the present!

In this case, I simply appealed to his better nature. How did it work out? It hasn't - yet. But I do know that if I had made him wrong, I would have lost any chance of recouping those expenses, and we wouldn't still be talking. Which means making him wrong in and of itself would have been ineffective, aka wrong!

Questions 5.3

1   What is usually true when you say someone "should" have done something?

2   When you think someone else is wrong, who does this create stress or pain for?

3   How effective is the strategy of letting someone else know that they are wrong?

4   But what if they really are wrong?

5   Explore the shoulds and the should-nots that you have in your life. Which do you hold for yourself and about others? Write them down for your own private use.

• - - - - - - • - - - - - •

Yes, but what's the next step?

If you see anything here in this koan that looks familiar, or speaks to your heart, it suggests your self-sabotage mechanism may mislead you in this manner. What can you do about it? There are many possibilities, but one effective strategy which has stood the test of time is to address the root of the problem.

Make a list of any shoulds and shouldn'ts that you currently have. Whenever you hear yourself say or think the word should, remind yourself that you are disagreeing with reality, and the universe is bigger, stronger than you. Life always wins, so just don't should anyone or anything!

• - - - - - - • - - - - - - - - - • - - - - - •

5.4   Being positive about the negative

The restaurant was classy, white linen, and large crystal wine glasses. The food was outstanding, just as it had been last time. In the best area in downtown Toronto, its reputation was well deserved. Yet, I was feeling disappointed rather than happy!

Since our sales results had been outstanding, dinner was to celebrate as well as to motivate us to continue producing. The Sales Director of the US company had flown in specially to meet us.

In one of our conversations earlier he had mentioned he had a case of some really lovely wine. At the time, I was an active member of both the Spanish as well as the American Wine Societies, I was really into wine. I can't remember which wine he had, but it was one I was really excited to taste, so I let him know! I thought he'd then promised to bring a bottle for us to share - but he hadn't.

Although I was careful not to show it, I was upset, and instead ordered another nice wine from the classic wine menu. Then, as the meal finished, I insisted on paying, rather than let him do so as he wanted.

He tried to insist, but I determined I would prevail.

He had chosen to celebrate in his manner rather than in the way I wanted to celebrate. If he wasn't prepared to allow me to taste the wine I thought he'd agreed to bring, then I wanted nothing else from him. I would pay for everything - and I did.

• - - - - - • - - - - •

Up till now

This incident brought home several lessons, which I learned later, along with a very useful strategy. As Vernon Sanders Law has brilliantly observed:

> *"Experience is a hard teacher because she gives the test first, the lesson afterward."*

Reflection on what had happened enabled me to see that my behavior had not added to the evening. In fact, my subtle negativity had simply detracted from the desired result.

My insistence on doing it my way, among other unwholesome effects, was a waste - a waste of money, of time, of resources, of opportunity, although none were in any way serious. By paying for the meal, I did not "get even" or show him. My insistence, instead, cost me a little, and I felt miffed, disgruntled. I doubt that he was over the moon with the result either. Neither of us benefitted.

My negative reaction came from expecting him to provide the anticipated bottle of wine and the disappointment of learning that he had not. Unmet expectations are a very common source of upsets. I "know" that sulking doesn't help. I've learned this lesson many times, it's simply counter-productive. All kinds of negative reactions, not just sulking, just don't work. I guess I'm something of a masochist. I seem to repeat life's lessons. When will I really "get it?"

Fortunately, I was gentle in insisting on paying, and my behavior did not entirely spoil the evening. Nevertheless, it did not enhance the mood. And having a good time, enhancing the mood, was the point of the dinner.

Yet again, I realized that if things don't turn out the way we want them to, we benefit by accepting the good that's there rather than being critical about what we perceive to be missing.

Next time, I determined I would look at the positive rather than the negative. Yet how can we do this effectively? How do we refer to the negative without putting energy into it? Here's an example:

Up till now, I used to just follow the negative thoughts which came in most such situations. I would take grim satisfaction in how badly I'd been treated, how he'd let me down. How much better would both his, and my, life be if he had just done it my way?

Using the exact phrase, "Up till now..." enables us to discuss the past without putting energy into perpetuating it. Remember the koan, The Focus Principle - the Law of Attraction part Two, in Chapter Four? Putting energy into what we don't want just strengthens what we don't want. Reliving the past will just reproduce the past, which gives us More Of The Same! Generally not what we are looking for!

So, for example, rather than declaring, "I'm bad at remembering names" it's far more helpful instead to say, "Up till now, I used to be bad at remembering names." Between two statements, two ways of saying anything, one will give somewhat different results than another. So choose the method that gives you the result you prefer, refer to all unwanted behaviours in the past.

This statement, "Up till now..." says nothing about the present, which starts afresh every second. It gives us the space to change, which is so valuable when we are not producing the results we want. It suggests that our future will be different, that we can and will stop perpetuating the past. It helps us change our actions which then achieve different results in the future. Perhaps even add, "and I'm now getting better at..." Then we put in the effort to fulfill this commitment. Then we improve, and things get better.

Questions 5.4

1   *What does this story tell us about being negative?*

2.   *Who lost out from my negativity, my disgruntling?*

3   *How can we refer to negative behavior or circumstances without invoking the Law of Attraction to perpetuate them.*

4.   *What other benefits does being positive about the negative have?*

• - - - - - - • - - - - - •

Yes, but what's the next step?

If you see anything here in this koan that looks familiar, or speaks to your heart, it suggests your self-sabotage mechanism may mislead you in this manner. What can you do about it? There are many possibilities, but one effective strategy which has stood the test of time is to address the root of the problem.

Whenever we want to refer to the negative, preface it with the phrase, Up till Now. This stops us putting energy into what we don't want.

• - - - - - - • - - - - - - - • - - - - - • - - - - - •

6 MORE ABOUT THE SELF-SABOTAGE MECHANISM

6.1   The Wolves - an American Indian viewpoint

"It's damn cold tonight!" I said into the silence. And nobody replied!

My statement contributed nothing, an insignificant remark of no apparent consequence. But still, I had made it!

Yet speaking was against our agreement. Our instructions for the weekend were clear, very clear. Noble silence! No matter how tempted we were, we were not to speak. Our time here was to be in absolute silence - simply use it as practice in resisting mental pressure, the mental pressure exerted by the self sabotage mechanism.

But the mind's insistence on saying something - anything - had proven so strong that eventually I succumbed. I'd been feeding the black wolf forever, and it had become so powerful that I couldn't help myself!

● - - - - - - ● - - - - - - ●

Your black and white wolves

North American Indians say that we all have two wolves living inside us, a black wolf and a white wolf. The black wolf sabotages our progress, while the white wolf leads us to our true self.

We have been feeding both wolves since we were young, and the more we feed each wolf, the bigger it gets.

The bigger the black wolf gets, the stronger it becomes, and the more feeding it wants. Just like a crying baby, the sooner you give it what it wants, the more it learns to insist on your immediate attention whenever it wants it. Give in at your peril!

The size, the strength of each wolf inside you now depends on how much food you have given it in the past. The one that is larger has been getting more food, more energy, and more attention.

So the decisive question is, "Which wolf do you want to become larger, stronger?"

Which is to ask, "Which wolf are you going to feed at this point in time? - Right now?"

Questions 6.1

1   *What does this koan tell you about your mind?*

2   *Which of the two wolves is your self-sabotage mechanism?*

3   *How does each wolf get stronger?*

• - - - - - • - - - - - •

Yes, but what's the next step?

If you see anything here in this koan that looks familiar, or speaks to your heart, it suggests your self-sabotage mechanism may mislead you in this manner. What can you do about it? There are many possibilities, but one effective strategy which has stood the test of time is to address the root of the problem.

Before choosing any action, get into the habit of asking yourself, is this going to feed the black wolf, or will it give energy to the white wolf? Then listen to your own answer...

• - - - - - • - - - - - - • - - - - - • - - - - - •

6.2   Is the price too high?

"Where are you?" asked the cross voice on the phone. It was Harold - and indeed he had a right to be angry!

The cold winter's afternoon was getting on, it was 3.35 p.m., and my haircut had been scheduled for 3.30. I'd forgotten about it. Again. The second time within a couple of months! Yet I have a diary both on my computer and a paper one, as well as a mobile phone that can remind me. And it was only in my paper diary. I'd gotten involved in a long talk with my sister, it was her birthday, and since she lives in Hong Kong, we don't see each other very often.

How cross with myself I was! "You idiot," I told myself, along with a few other choice words. Now I know you wouldn't ever do something so silly, but I was now in a bad mood. At one time I would have beat myself up mentally. This time, I decided to put some energy into ensuring it didn't happen yet again.

A while ago, Harold had told me about some clients who didn't keep their appointments. "Then charge them," I had said. "They need to learn the lesson that your time is valuable." And now I'd forgotten one for the second time!

"I'll have to charge you for this missed appointment," said he, "that's the second time...'

"Yes," I had to agree, "that's fair."

I paid the price of not ensuring that my scheduling system really worked, even though my earlier misses (this wasn't the only time) made me realize it wasn't working properly. I've now put the next appointment in my phone, in addition to my paper diary. And the price was definitely higher - I had to pay double when he cut my hair later that week, as well as the time wasted in making another appointment.

Now I really know that my manual system is unreliable. Whenever appropriate I ensure my phone reminds me, so it's been a valuable lesson. I'll now make sure I take my own advice, and do what works, rather than what doesn't! So, for such a useful lesson, is the doubled price and the wasted time that it cost us both really too high?

. - - - - - . - - - - - .

Paying the Price

Everything has its price, which includes every new understanding, and all personal growth; in fact, all progress as well as all lack of progress. No exceptions! You cannot escape paying the price, there's no free lunch!

Many of us don't understand this, we want to avoid paying the price. This is one reason why we so often avoid new experiences and hence stagnate. But the price always gets paid eventually. By you. Yet you have full choice over when. Paying helps us value it, so I've learned to be glad we always pay!

You don't have to pay the price immediately, it may be deferred until later, even lots later. Perhaps even another lifetime. Long-term, the universe is in perfect balance, you don't get something for nothing. Every imbalance is eventually corrected. Unhealthy habits always catch up with you, as Henry found out in Is there really a Most Important Question, see Chapter Three.

Just like at the bank, every price you defer paying will carry interest. It's always more costly later on. Yet the price you pay may not be the same that someone else pays for the same thing, and the price is not necessarily measured in money.

This is just another way of recognizing that there are consequences to every action.

Questions 6.2

1. *What does this koan tell you about something that appears to be free?*

2. *Does this mean that there are always consequences?*

3. *How do you benefit by paying the price now?*

• - - - - - - • - - - - - •

Yes, but what's the next step?

If you see anything here in this koan that looks familiar, or speaks to your heart, it suggests your self-sabotage mechanism may mislead you in this manner. What can you do about it? There are many possibilities, but one effective strategy which has stood the test of time is to address the root of the problem.

There's always a price. So, when deciding on any action, first ask yourself; am I willing to pay the price? In general, the sooner you pay it the better.

• - - - - - - • - - - - - • - - - - - • - - - - - •

6.3   The real value of Distractions

"The couch is dirty, it needs recovering," said Wanda. "Yes," agreed Linda, her fifteen year-old daughter.

It was just before Christmas. The couch was indeed dirty, and it did need recovering. They also needed a computer at home, and the two issues were competing for the same money - they were on a budget. The computer would enable her to work at home, send emails without going to an Internet café, and Linda would be able to do her homework on the computer as well. The couch just didn't look good.

But the dirty couch was very visibly in front of her, while the computer was just a very good idea. The couch would look so good in new white fabric, envisaged Wanda, as she thought about the guests she'd invited for Christmas.

The computer would be so useful, she dreamt, but then she remembered her friends coming around. It's so important to look good. So she recovered the couch in white, which required her to take a one month Christmas hiatus in her car repayments.

Barely six months later, the couch again needed cleaning, and the computer was still a much needed fantasy.

. - - - - - . - - - - - .

Distractions and Temptations

Distractions and temptations are just diversions from achieving what we have set out to do.

Every time Wanda now looks at her couch, it reminds her of the temptation that she yielded to despite her better judgment. Now she can use the couch as feedback, to help her resist temptation and distraction.

A temptation suggests that something else is even more desirable than our current intention. It works by making something else look so appealing, we're led toward it. No matter how much a man may love his wife, many find temptation does occur, especially when faced with an available hot young thing!

Distractions, on the other hand, take us away from something that we may be deceived into thinking is not very desirable. A distraction denigrates our current plan, implying it's less attractive and luring us away from our current goal. At university, I found it difficult to resist the many distractions that invariably seemed to come up when homework beckoned. Could my lack of self-discipline have had any connection to my lack of academic success?

Neither distractions nor temptations are bad, they simply are what they are. They are attempts by the ssm to divert us from our current focus. Diversions take energy. Energy away from achieving the results that our present direction will bring. When we allow ourselves to be distracted or tempted, our goal becomes deferred and less likely. This help us stay where we are - tends to give us More Of The Same. Better to avoid them both.

The ssm will try to steer us away from a worthwhile goal, that's its job. It'll try to sabotage our efforts by telling us that there's something wrong with the goal, or the methodology, or another person, or that we're moving too slowly, or whatever!

When real change starts happening, usually a few months into learning to cope with self-sabotage, then the stress, the suffering involved will start to surface. And the ssm may then start playing the Blame Game. It'll try and get you emoting, or your mind to think that it's someone else's fault, anyone else's fault - but not yours!

Yet the unhappiness, the suffering, the stress is internal, because that's where the problem is. So be forewarned, beware of rationalizations, be aware.

Questions 6.3

1   *What are temptations and distractions?*

2   *When we allow ourselves to be distracted or tempted, what happens?*

3   *How best to cope with temptations and distractions?*

• - - - - - - • - - - - - •

Yes, but what's the next step?

If you see anything here in this koan that looks familiar, or speaks to your heart, it suggests your self-sabotage mechanism may mislead you in this manner. What can you do about it? There are many possibilities, but one effective strategy which has stood the test of time is to address the root of the problem.

When tempted, or distraction beckons, recognize that movement away from your goal is unlikely to help you realize it. So come to real clarity about the importance of your goals - in advance. Then keep choosing the same thing.

• - - - - - - • - - - - - - - - - • - - - - - - • - - - - - •

6.4   Just here to help you!

I had to laugh. It was a warm summer's day in London, many years ago, and I had just resolved a very frustrating argument with Donald, my boss. What was so funny was his reaction. Even though I had stopped arguing and said I understood his viewpoint, he kept insisting he was right...

It had started out as a disagreement, and soon turned into an argument. I can't even remember what it was about! Donald insisted that something was so, and I said it was not. His insistence was so frustrating, why couldn't he understand my perspective?

Even when he had persuaded me that his viewpoint was valid, and I eventually understood his perspective, I declined to agree with him. The more he insisted he was right - and he insisted he was right most of the time - the more I dug my heels in. Eventually, we agreed to differ and I left his office to climb the narrow stairs to mine.

As I climbed the stairs, I reflected on what had just happened. I saw how obstinate I was being, and realized that arguing was just a waste of time and energy. I didn't like the unpleasant, frustrated way I felt when arguing. Why do it? I asked myself. I now understood his perspective, and realized why he thought he was right.

As soon as I reached my office, the phone rang. It was Donald, still very frustrated. He wasn't going to let me get away with it!

"I'm right and you're wrong!" he insisted. His obnoxious manner tempted me to continue the argument. But I now understood his perspective.

"Yes, you're right," I replied. He didn't hear me.

"This is the way it is, and I'm right, you're wrong," he repeated.

"You are right," said I, "I now get what you're saying and you are right."

We went round the loop yet a third time before he realized I was now agreeing with him.

"I'm what?" he eventually said.

"You are right," I repeated yet again. "I agree with you."

Since I had stopped disagreeing with him, there was no more resistance, and he had nothing to push against. "Well, of course I'm right," he said weakly and, yet again, I agreed that he was right.

It's even funnier in retrospect than it was at the time. When I stopped resisting, and stopped being frustrated, he had nothing to push against. The lack of resistance put him totally off balance. The argument ended when I understood his perspective and became willing to let him know that.

• - - - - - - • - - - - - •

Frustration

Frustration is a very common tool the self-sabotage mechanism uses to allow us to experience the lack of what we really want. To do its job and give us an experience of scarcity.

Frustrations clearly show us that there are changes which need to be made. That's all. Yet where do we usually see the cause of the frustration? How often do we view the cause as what's outside - rather than what's inside, or a combination of both.

The outside world is what it is and, no matter how many times we try and change it to exactly what we want, we often aren't that successful. Even when we do succeed, it rarely lasts that long. I know this only too well, I've tried so many times throughout my life!

The most effective change, of course, is in our perspective, the way we view things, rather than only in what's happening outside. A change in understanding is internal, and far more permanent.

In fact, the only thing which we do have real control over is the inside! Yet how many of us make the effort to manage our context, our inside space, properly? Since the frustration, the pain is inside our heads, then that's the place to make the change.

So the constructive way to deal with frustrations is to exercise control over the way we look at things. Find a more powerful perspective, think with intent and ignore the random thoughts that just arise. Choose our thoughts in the same way that we choose our actions. Exercise your choice in what to think about.

This new understanding enables us to manage our thoughts, and our reactions. Our temperament improves since our emotions also benefit from the change.

Questions 6.4

1   What is true about frustration?

2   Who has to change to relieve your frustration?

3   How can you use frustration to benefit you?

4   Discuss Donald's ssm in the story.

● - - - - - ● - - - - - ●

Yes, but what's the next step?

If you see anything here in this koan that looks familiar, or speaks to your heart, it suggests your self-sabotage mechanism may mislead you in this manner. What can you do about it? There are many possibilities, but one effective strategy which has stood the test of time is to address the root of the problem.

Whenever you're frustrated, remember that frustration is a call to action. But the action required is internal, not external as the self sabotage mechanism may try and persuade you to think!

Life - reality - is just what it is. The tension in your internal perspective on reality is causing your frustration. How do we know that? Since the frustration is internal, that's where the problem is! So ask yourself which internal change would eliminate your frustration? Then implement that change to your viewpoint. This revitalized and refreshed context will help eliminate your frustration, and you'll be more in tune with life.

● - - - - - - ● - - - - - - - - - - ● - - - - - - - - ● - - - - - - ●

6.5   A place of real calm and joy

In total amazement I stared at it. Removing the pill from the blister pack had broken it in two! It had never happened before, and it's never happened since. Yet this was exactly what I needed to see!

I was out of town for a while, and hadn't planned properly. I had four days to go, and the anti-inflammatory pills I take daily had almost run out. There were only two pills left.

What shall I do, I wondered as I realized my predicament. Take one every second day? Go without at the end and suffer? The dilemma was interesting.

The next morning, it was time to take my anti-inflammatory. I had just finished shaving, and fumbled with the pack when the pill broke in two. What a wonderful coincidence, my mind told me. Then I realized! This was no coincidence, the universe had answered my question for me.

● - - - - - - ● - - - - - - ●

The observer

Our intuition, our inner knowing, our vibe offers us sure guidance - yet never minds if we ignore it. This is also known as our still small voice of calm, and it is indeed small and still. It's tough to hear it when the ssm is shouting or insisting.

Whenever we choose to let the ssm go, we can just observe from a place of calmness and clarity, some call this the witness. Then we can listen to our intuition, and we see that the universe is on our side.

This is when we are at our most effective. We know what needs to be done, we don't waste our energy emoting, we just handle it. Things happen to assist us. We can even enlist others to assist us into fulfilling the task at hand, without ordering them about or being egotistical.

There's a feeling of clarity and calmness. We are at peace and enjoy life and those around us. Others will see us just getting on with the job, and may compliment us on how well we're handling things.

If you've experienced this, then you know it's an amazing space to be in. If you haven't, you have a real treat coming!

Questions 6.5

1.   *What is your intuition?*

2.   *When are you most effective?*

3.   *How will you know when the ssm is no longer in complete charge?*

· - - - - - - · - - - - - ·

Yes, but what's the next step?

If you see anything here in this koan that looks familiar, or speaks to your heart, it suggests your self-sabotage mechanism may mislead you in this manner. What can you do about it? There are many possibilities, but one effective strategy which has stood the test of time is to address the root of the problem.

Whenever your vibe, your intuition, suggests you do something, remember it's on your side - and do it. Although perhaps not immediately, you'll benefit in the long-term!

· - - - · - - - - · - - - - - · - - - - - ·

7 WHERE DO I GO FROM HERE?

7.1   Yet another concert!

The tickets looked interesting, it was a concert I did want to hear. Yet I also wanted to relax, just do nothing in particular, to have some time for myself. I didn't feel like going out, I needed a night off!

Both classical music and opera enthralled me, I was an enthusiastic fan and had been purchasing seasons tickets for several years. I would receive information on all the concerts for the upcoming seasons well in advance, which meant I'd bought these tickets a year or so earlier.

The previous year I had let my enthusiasm run away with me. I selected all those that seemed interesting, and purchased a pair of tickets as usual, to take a friend with me. That must have been a dozen or so series.

Come the end of February, I'd had enough. It wasn't that the concerts weren't enjoyable, rather that I'd been out every night. Or what seemed like every night. Twenty concerts already this month, I just didn't feel like making the effort to go to yet another. But waste the money? So I invited yet another friend and went.

The concert was superb, well worth the effort. I purchased a couple of CD's and even got the performer to sign them.

Yet although I enjoyed all the music, I was just doing too much. I had no unscheduled time for myself. The following year I made sure I subscribed to no more than a concert a week. I had realized that it was possible to have too much of a good thing, no matter how good the good thing is.

Now I don't subscribe to concert series, although I still enjoy both classical music and opera. I've stopped rushing around frantically. I now have the time to enjoy unscheduled time every day as well as to complete all my commitments to the spirit as well as the letter. How? By eliminating some admittedly very desirable activities. Rather than obey a hectic schedule, I prefer being able to do what I feel like doing. True freedom can be seen as having the space to enjoy being spontaneous.

New commitments I now consider very carefully. I've learned to ask the vital questions:

- Do I really need the results that doing it will bring?

- Even more compellingly, can I afford the time it will take?

- What will I let go of to find that time?

- If I have actually enough money at the moment, why do I believe my mind when it tells me I need even more?

- Which is primary, my family, my wife and kids - or the extra income that working more will give me?

Now I know that enjoyment of the journey, of the moment, is more Important than reaching that apparently desirable goal. I've slowed down to enjoy the flowers along the way. If the sunset is particularly beautiful, I stop and watch. This rarely delays me for more than a few minutes, and if it makes me late for something, then I'm late. Life's too short to worry about what isn't. I prefer to enjoy what is.

• - - - - - • - - - - - •

Living at redline

As we've seen throughout this book, problems come whenever we automatically believe our thoughts. So I have consciously chosen to stop being gullible. The technique is to check out whatever the mind tells you to ascertain if it really is true. This means all thoughts! I've learned to ask myself the fundamental questions:

- Can I afford the time?

- Do I really need the results?

- What am I willing to give up to make time for something new, since I'm already spending all twenty-four hours each and every day?

- When do I really enjoy myself?

- Why am I spending my time doing this?

- What do I want to do right now?

And I now know that "Right now, nothing!" is an answer that does serve me, since we all need some time just for ourselves every day.

I had been living at redline. But living at redline is not sustainable long-term. Living at redline comes from believing your mind when it says you need more, or that you should. This is the path to yuppie flu and nervous breakdowns.

What is redline? A Formula One racing car is designed to run at redline - maximum

- for one hundred percent of the time. After every race, and there's a race every week or two, the team takes each car completely apart and rebuilds it. Including testing, the car and the engine only last   around ten hours or so. Why? Because running at redline is very stressful, and if it revs past redline, it over-stresses.

In 2006, new rules required a F1 engine to last for two races instead of just one. Until they relaxed this new rule change, the teams just didn't practice as much. If the engine blew up, the driver got pushed lower down the starting grid, a severe penalty.

In contrast, we run our road cars at a small fraction of potential. Rarely do we floor the accelerator, or need to brake at maximum. As a result, they last far longer, more like ten years than ten hours.

Yet how many of us try and squeeze the maximum out of life, thinking that doing more and having more is always the same as enjoying ourselves? Sometimes more is less (think about this one very carefully!) Do you want to model your life on a Formula One racing car, or would you rather have many more years to enjoy?

Neither is wrong, yet our approach, our context, will give us very different consequences. And some consequences are more desirable than others. When you really get this, your life will really take off. It is indeed entirely up to you to avoid suffering and arduous circumstances.

It's said that, "The only true freedom comes from discipline." This freedom comes directly, it comes from direct control. But contrary to the assumption most of us make, it's discipline over what we think we should do. It's control over our internal landscape, rather than control over the outside circumstances, that makes the real difference!

Questions 7.1

1.   *Why can running at redline be detrimental?*
2.   *Is it possible to have too much of a good thing?*
3.   *Is it possible to do too much of a good thing?*
4.   *When do you have true freedom?*
5.   *If you're running at redline now, what are some of the fundamental questions that you may not have asked yourself, or whose answers you may be ignoring?*

● - - - - - - ● - - - - - ●

Yes, but what's the next step?

If you see anything here in this koan that looks familiar, or speaks to your heart, it suggests your self-sabotage mechanism may mislead you in this manner. What can you do about it? There are many possibilities, but one effective strategy which has stood the test of time is to address the root of the problem.

When your mind tells you that everything is important, or that everything is urgent, remember this is actually impossible. They say that when everything is important, nothing's important! This just means you haven't prioritized, or remembered, what is important for you. Then just do whatever this remembering suggests...

· - - - · - - - - · - - - - · - - - - · - - - - ·

7.2 Was she pulling my leg?

"Oh, bother!" said I. Actually, those aren't quite the exact words I used. The car was in the ditch, and I had driven it there. Deliberately!

My girlfriend, Jane, and I were on holiday. We were staying in a rather nice resort up in the country, and had gone for a drive to enjoy the scenery. It was the Canadian winter and there was fresh snow everywhere.

We had been chatting happily and she mentioned how deceiving appearances can be. "For example," she said, "the side of the road looks so solid with its covering of snow, yet there's a ditch between the road and the fence."

"Really," said I, having trouble disbelieving the evidence of my eyes.

"There always is," she told me, "that's the way we do it here."

Although I was raised in town, I don't know that much about the countryside, and I was fairly new to Canada, this didn't make any sense to me. Was she telling the truth, or should I believe what my eyes and my mind were telling me?

"Are you sure?" I asked. It seemed unlikely. The verge of the road looked so solid and safe. Could she be joshing me?

"There's a ditch there," she laughed . Yet the more she insisted, and the more she laughed, the more I doubted her.

"Let's check it out," said I, sure that I was right in doubting what she was saying. In fact, so convinced was I of being right that I turned the steering wheel and drove gently onto to the very solid-looking verge.

But appearances can be deceiving. In fact, they often are! What a valuable lesson to learn about doubt! We were stuck in a ditch in the middle of nowhere.

A few minutes later, a passing car stopped. We were lucky. It turned out to be the local farmer whose tractor was nearby. Less than an hour later, we were back on our way. No damage done, except to my ego and my beliefs around doubt and the reliability of my thoughts.

• - - - - - • - - - - - •

Doubt

Automatically believing our thoughts can get us into serious trouble! Back then I didn't investigate all thoughts to see which ones were true, to ask what might be reasonable under the circumstances. What was even more relevant, I didn't think to ascertain the truth in such a way as to minimize any possible harm or damage. I was so convinced the verge was solid that I didn't even bother to check it out by walking on it.

But unpacked snow is not solid. Jane was right and the doubts, the thoughts I'd had were wrong. The ditch in the middle of nowhere gave me my proof.

Scientists and the scientific method start with doubt. They continue doubting until the point at which doubt vanishes, and then they know instead.

Doubt can be divided into two types. Doubt about the outside, how things are - the facts. And doubt about the inside - our thoughts - what it means.

Doubt about the facts, about what happened outside, how things work, is productive initially. When we acknowledge we don't have all the answers, this motivates us to keep looking. Living in the question is healthy. Yet, once we've investigated and do know the facts, then doubt stops being productive, it just wastes our time and energy.

Doubt about our thoughts is also healthy, it's vital not to believe the mind automatically. So also start by doubting all thoughts, don't be gullible. Inquire to see which thoughts are true for us. Do they fit in with what we already know? Yet just as outside, once we've inquired and come to know that something is our truth then it's time to stop doubting.

We're discussing doubt about both inner and outer truth here. Once you've come to see what's true for you, then it's time to trust yourself. We don't believe in believing; when you know, belief is unnecessary.

Doubt about the truth is one of the self sabotage mechanism's more common strategies to feed off your energy. It wants you to believe that all its thoughts are true, yet wants you to doubt your truth. This is exactly backward. Rather doubt it and its thoughts and believe what you've already investigated and know to be your truth.

The ssm wants you to doubt if your truths, your realizations and breakthroughs really are true! Yet when you originally checked them out, you saw that they were your truth at the time. And if you re-examine them very carefully, you'll see they are still your truth.

But the ssm still questions, it wants to leave you uncertain. It insists, "Believe me, but doubt yourself, doubt your truth, doubt the conclusion of your thorough investigation, doubt your own experiences, doubt your path forward." This is self-sabotage. Doubt, negativity, uncertainty... all designed to give you a negative outcome in the future. All food for the black wolf. As William Shakespeare said so many years ago:

> *'Our doubts are traitors, and make us lose the good we oft might win by fearing to attempt.'*

So, once you've decided on something, eliminate the doubt. First inquire, check into it thoroughly, and once you know your truth then recognize that you know. You don't need to believe when you know instead. Then you can trust yourself.

Doubt is the ssm trying to sabotage you. As was my feeling of I'm right, and therefore what my girlfriend was telling me must be wrong. This is the value of initially being skeptical. We stay open-minded and check out the other side of a story even when it seems wrong. Then we integrate the new perspective and thereby gain even more power from our newly transcended perspective.

Questions 7.2

1. *What does the scientific method have to do with doubt?*
2. *Discuss the two types of doubt. How do they differ?*
3. *Why does the ssm want you to doubt?*
4. *What's so funny about the ssm's use of doubt?*

• - - - - - • - - - - - •

Yes, but what's the next step?

If you see anything here in this koan that looks familiar, or speaks to your heart, it suggests your self-sabotage mechanism may mislead you in this manner. What can you do about it? There are many possibilities, but one effective strategy which has stood the test of time is to address the root of the problem.

Whenever doubt comes up, get into the habit of asking yourself, how likely this is to be real? Is it plausible? Have I already investigated this?

Or could it be the self sabotage mechanism attempting to sabotage your progress? If you're already in the habit of investigating your thoughts, you know that self sabotage is the more likely answer...

• - - - - - - • - - - - - - - • - - - - - - - • - - - - - •

7.3   What's in store for you...

Some of the perspectives we've offered in this introduction to self-sabotage will be very familiar to you. And some will be rather new.

This is just the start of your journey. Overcoming the self-sabotage mechanism needs ongoing effort. Most of these koans have a lot more depth, extra levels with much extra personal power. We've only scratched the surface here. Personal growth is a personal matter, just like an exercise program, you can't delegate the effort required. As a plant flowers from within, using the sunlight and food provided by nature, people also blossom with the right resources.

So what resources do we provide as you continue to invest in understanding, recognizing, and learning to cope effectively with the self-sabotage mechanism?

Just a few among the many more koans we'll be exploring are:

-        What Choice will you make this time?
-        I'll do it... tomorrow!
-        Gullible? Cynical? Or Skeptical?
-        Negative emotions are so... helpful?
-        New Thinking, new Willingness, new Effectiveness!
-        Dealing with it - proactively!
-        Revenge is sweet. Or is it?

-        What do you really want?

If you'd rather spend more time succeeding, and less time failing, then you'll find your investment in studying what does work - and what doesn't - to be tremendously rewarding. What better way to experience the consequences of failure than by outsourcing the effort, by delegating rather than suffering personally?

Yet you will still need to really know them, rather than just know about them - that's another universal law to explore in more detail. So if you wish to avoid the suffering involved in failing personally, you'll want to know time-tested strategies which work.

We all have a choice. Either continue to allow the self-sabotage mechanism to negatively influence our lives, or we can learn to overcome it. Eventually, most of us choose the latter. At some point in your life, you'll probably become so fed up with the unsatisfactory results the self-sabotage mechanism continues to bring that you'll start this course gladly. Most of us get to that point eventually and then we learn to improve our context. Yet the time at which you choose to cease your self-sabotage is entirely optional, you have full control over when.

But why choose the consequences of continuing self-sabotage? Rather enjoy the full benefits available to you by learning to run your own life now. Rather become more powerful, more effective, more at peace with yourself and the world by choosing the full extra personal power now available to you. Decide to continue learning to overcome the self-sabotage mechanism.

• - - - - - • - - - - - • - - - - - • - - - - •

7.4   The Next Step

Of course, you now know that the koans which we've started exploring in this book are just your first pass at the immense extra personal power available. The tip of the iceberg. Most koans have extra levels which expand upon the changes discussed to further improve your context. And changing your context is what personal growth is really all about.

Yet many people don't want to change their perspective , they instead prefer to change what they're doing. Then, within a few years, they find themselves back in the same situation facing the same challenges even though the faces and the places are different. Society teaches us to focus on what to do, yet what you do can only change the outside circumstances. Whereas inside is the place where you feel happy or unhappy, satisfied or uneasy, in harmony with life or discontented. The inside, rather than the outside, is the place to put your attention.

Without a commitment to change internally, nothing much can change. Yet everyone asks, "What should I do?" Rather ask the far more powerful question, "How can I increase my personal power? How can I change my context?" This is the question that holds the key to achieving what you really want. As Jim Rohn sagely says,

> *"If the idea of having to change ourselves makes us uncomfortable, we can remain as we are. We can choose rest over labor, entertainment over education, delusion over truth, and doubt over confidence. The choices are ours to make. But while we curse the effect, we continue to nourish the cause."*

Wayne Dyer uses rather less words to say much the same thing:

> *"When you change the way you look at things, the things you look at change!"*

When you really want different results, benefit from the help available to change the things that need changing.

It's been a fascinating exercise deciding what to include in this short introduction to the role that self-sabotage has in all our lives - and especially in mine!

My life seemed to move from one less than satisfactory consequence to another, and I've now come to the uncomfortable realization that the self-sabotage mechanism is working all the time. It's been a constant guiding force in my life, and I've spent years learning the discipline required to overcome it. Unless you've spent some time being totally honest with yourself, you may not realize how much the self-sabotage mechanism attempts to run your life. Have you noticed the extent to which it's been one of the guiding forces in your life? Self-sabotage could be the main reason why you may not quite be living the life you'd really love to live. To quote Emile Henry Gauvreau, don't be any part of

> *'that strange race of people aptly described as spending their lives doing things they detest to make money they don't want to buy things they don't need to impress people they dislike.'*

This appetizer introduces the concept of self sabotage by looking at around twenty of the many hundreds of koans. With a change in strategy, you've seen how you can resist the tendency to self-sabotage. And how, by changing your thinking - changing your context - you can enjoy more desirable consequences.

Did you just avoid spending time on one particular koan, because you know that it's going to change your life in an unwanted fashion? Yup, I've also tried that! Yet such avoidance can often be often the self-sabotage mechanism trying to duck what can help launch a whole new life. For me, what helps is to focus on the benefits that change can bring, instead of the disruption that it can cause. Rather choose to have a major boost, decide to put some attention on increasing your personal power to bring you the results you want.

There's always a price to pay and if we avoid paying it now, it's generally more expensive later!

Any negativity you may feel is due to the self-sabotage mechanism. And right now, it may well be working hard to persuade you to go no further. So the decisive question to contemplate is, What am I going to do now?

The average person will just yawn, and continue doing what he's doing now. And nothing will change.

Some people will tell themselves that they should do something about this tomorrow, but right now they're too busy. And they'll ignore the fact that tomorrow never comes.

And a few - those who want real change in their life - will remind themselves of their answer to the Most Important Question, see Chapter Three. They decide they want the results that doing it will bring. Remember that wonderful quotation from the musical production of "Time":

"Your life is an expression of your mind. You are the creator of your own universe, for as a human being, you are free to will whatever state of being you desire through the use of your thoughts and words. There is great power there."

Is it worth it? I hear you ask. Perhaps your mind is telling you that you can't afford it, it costs too much. Yet the ssm doesn't ask - compared to what? So compare this investment in improving your capabilities to something expensive, say a new car. The happiness a new car brings fades after a while, while its usefulness is limited to getting around. A few years later, it's time to replace it again.

Yet the benefits of resolving your internal challenges, of learning to make real choices never fade. Which would you rather have, a new car, or increased personal power? As you change your context and become more capable at resolving the challenges of life, the joy that you experience can be intense and the benefits continue forever. As Benjamin Franklin famously said:

"If a man empties his purse into his head, no one can take it from him."

If this makes sense to you, then just click here.

Will it work? is another significant question. Perhaps you have gotten used to the situation you're in, and have rationalized it as - better the devil you know than the devil you don't. The ssm can always come up with a "What if" worse than your current situation. One of the numerous objections it comes up with might be, I'm different; it won't work for me. Then, in comparison, your current situation doesn't seem that bad. When it gives us this specious answer, just remember that the job of the ssm is to get you to sabotage your progress. And all progress involves change! In fact, it's tough to progress without change! (:-) smile, big smile.) One of my favorite quotations about changing your context is by that incredibly prolific author - A. N. Onymous:

"To make a change in your life, you have to make a change in your life."

Or perhaps it's got your mind to tell you that you can't afford it. And that may indeed be true. You may not have the money right now, or the time. But this fails to realize that your outer circumstances simply reflect your inner state. The powerful question to ask if the ssm has given you this thought is, can I afford NOT to invest the money or the time in myself?

Without changing your inner state, there can be no real, lasting change to your outer circumstances. So instead of looking at the lack, the negative, rather ask yourself, how could I find the money or the time? This opens up the space of possibility and allows a more positive answer to surface.

But will it be hard? is another reason to procrastinate that the ssm sometimes gives. Maybe, and maybe not; again it depends on you. On your attitude, your willingness to change, how positive you are, and your answer to the paramount question, Do I want the results that doing it will bring. In five years time, either you'll have made a change in your life, or not. Either way, you'll be five years older!

Yet we now know that dissatisfaction, discomfort, pain, and suffering are simply messages. They tell us, for our own sake, that we need to change something. When the suffering is in your head, that's where the change is needed. If you need the message to be clearer, then no problem, life will oblige! It will make it more intense. It'll keep increasing the volume until you can ignore it no longer. So don't keep suffering, rather decide to deal with it now.

Or maybe you are one of the select few who has decided that you do want a real change in your life. You are willing to take responsibility for making that change and to invest in what will make tomorrow different. Why? Because you want the results, the amazing benefits, that doing it will bring! As Robert Kiyosaki says in his own inimitable style:

> *"If you want to be rich, you first need to work on your context, more than on what you do.... you must first change your context. That is why I recommend you... continually work on upgrading your context. Remember it is your context... that becomes your reality, regardless of what you do."*

Will your life be better tomorrow?

It can be - if you're prepared to take action today. If so, you already know the value of prioritizing your time and your money. And the most worthwhile investment you can make? In yourself! When you invest in your personal growth you can never lose!

Then you already recognize that your actions today create your circumstances tomorrow, and making the internal changes to your context today is the only thing that makes any real change in tomorrow.

And then you will join those who live the life of their wildest dreams. Although you may, or may not, achieve the wealth of Bill Gates, or Robert Kiyosaki, or John Templeton, the richness of your life will give you the peace, love, calm and joy that we all seek.

· - - - - - - · - - - - - - · - - - - - · - - - - - ·

8 QUESTIONS AND ANSWERS

Questions and Answers 1

Questions and Answers 1.1

1   Tell us more about you.

See About the author below

There's also a short bio on this web-page

Questions and Answers 1.2

1   What is this book about?

Its purpose is to introduce you to the deception of the self-sabotage mechanism, to learn when it operates and how to avoid its blandishments. The true stories here tell you when I've listened to the ssm, and how the circumstances that generally followed were undesirable.

So don't repeat my mistakes, make your own! :-)

2   How do deception and falsehood differ from truth?

Deception and falsehood are not truth, nor are they the opposite of truth. The ssm would love you to see deception as the opposite of truth, because with that recognition comes energy. And the ssm feeds on energy, as does the rest of the world.

Just as darkness is the absence of light - rather than its opposite - falsity is simply the absence of truth. This crucial distinction gives no recognition to deception, thereby avoiding giving it any energy or focus.

3.   Is the self-sabotage mechanism right, bad, or wrong?

No. There is nothing in this text that will suggest that the self-sabotage mechanism is right, bad, or wrong. Or even that falsity, or being deceived, is right, bad or wrong.

To get the complete picture, you need to experience all sides of each incident, each event. The ssm's job is to give you the side that you wouldn't willingly choose. But it certainly does have undesirable consequences.

This is not to say that deception is effective in getting you to where you want to be. On the contrary, unless you accurately know your current position, which means you know where you are truly - rather than falsely - any path you take from here is unlikely to get you there. The path suggested by deception is merely ineffective. Yet many people confound, confuse wrong with ineffective, and don't see the essential difference.

When we decline to judge - refuse to make something wrong - then we avoid putting energy into judging, into being wrong, and hence avoid using the Law of Attraction against us. See the whole of chapter Four for lots more on this critically important perspective.

Questions and Answers 1.3

1   What is the Magic Pill that gives you whatever you want to be, do, or have; no matter what it is.

Do what works to get you that. Don't do what doesn't work.

This seems so simple, does it really work? Yes, indeed! People confuse simple and easy, they think the two mean the same, but they don't. The simplest things can be so very difficult. See If it's simple, it must be easy, in Chapter Three.

2   Are there any other incisive strategies to help you get wherever you want to be?

Yes, many. Learn not to trust the self-sabotage mechanism. Which means only believe a thought once you've investigated it first. Then you're more likely to see when your mind is not telling you the truth!

Recognize that simple does not mean easy.

Listen to your still small voice, your intuition.

Know where you are now.

This book is full of such strategies. So read on.

3   Why is clarity in thinking vital?

Clarity in thinking is crucial because the less clarity we have, the less accurately we know our current position and what is so right now. Then the ssm has more scope to deceive us about a viable path forward.

Questions and Answers 1.4

1   Since facts are facts, why don't other people share our truths?

Facts are external, what happened. Whereas even when the content is the same, our internal perspective on a given fact may be different to another person. And their context will be different in some way, no matter how small, to ours. Our truth depends on our context as well as the content.

2   What's crucial about accuracy?

The more accuracy about the facts of the matter, the more likely is the path you take to get you to your goal.

And inaccuracy is ineffective. It may not work.

Take the example given, you want to drive to Los Angeles. Should you drive north, or south? Suppose you are with someone who believes you are in San Diego, yet you believe you are in San Francisco. If you cannot resolve your factual differences , you may have problems...

3   What enabled Robert Kiyosaki to gain millions of dollars from that real-estate tape.

His willingness to be open-minded.

Open-mindedness, especially when we do not agree with a different perspective, is the key to gaining extra power.

If we don't yet understand a new perspective, or we disagree with it, that lack of insight simply makes its extra power unavailable to us. That's why Robert was willing to put in the time and energy to actually "get it."

Questions and Answers 1.5

1.   What do we suggest as indispensable here?

To learn the rules that govern the results, so you can create your life the way you really want it.

2.   When might you not know what you really want?

Your ssm might have stepped in and got you to believe that you want what it wants instead.

You may think that you want something, but until you've really investigated that thought, and contemplated the result, how do you know whether or not this really is an outcome you desire.

Or you may not have decided what you want in life yet, it's premature. No sweat, you're just not there yet, although the ssm may try to persuade you this is a serious problem.

3.   How do you gain the power to improve all aspects of your situation?

By embracing new perspectives, changing your context, transcending the limitations of your current beliefs, learning how self-sabotage works, and coming to know your truth.

Questions and Answers 1.6

1.   What is a koan?

A new way of looking at an incident, a situation, even a phrase. A different perspective, a more powerful viewpoint, a change in understanding about life and how it works. A distinction that can help you become more effective in a situation.

Koans increase your ability to manage your context, your internal world. Being entirely rational, they act to eliminate confusion.

2.   Why is it paramount that you do more than just understand a koan?

So that you can access the extra strength inherent in its new perspective.

Many people feel a surge of energy when they first understand - "get" - a koan, that's a foretaste of the increase in power that it holds for you. Yet you can only access this power by first integrating it and then putting it to work.

3.   How will the self-sabotage mechanism deal with all this?

Self-sabotage comes in many forms. Stress, emotional discomfort, disagreements... Basically all the amazing varied forms of negativity may be the self-sabotage mechanism.

Even perfectly valid questions dealing with more complex issues can be self-sabotage. The problem is not with the validity of such questions. It's the insistence of the ssm that they have to be answered right now, its unwillingness to wait until you can walk before you try and run.

It may try and dilute your attention with questions such as "'what if... ?" and "supposing that... ?'" All temptations and diversions are aimed at stopping you getting real clear on what you're learning right now. No matter how essential they may be to cover in the future, they can be left until you know more. Right now, you are here and now, not in the future!

Be warned, the self-sabotage mechanism is very subtle and very, very devious. It has to be, since all its strategies are designed to stop you changing and bring you undesirable circumstances.

4.   *Is what is written here to be taken as gospel?*

Not at all! On the contrary, check out everything we suggest, explore for yourself and find out what works for you. If it doesn't work, then it's not for you. Your truth is your internal perspective on a matter, whereas facts are external. When you know what your truth is, there is no need to believe what someone else says. So don't believe, rather put in the energy to know. Then you can't be manipulated!

So no, this book is not gospel. It's an incisive basic guide in getting you to analyze your thoughts, to think for yourself, and thereby to discover what does work for you. And what doesn't!

Questions and Answers 2

Questions and Answers 2.1

1   Who finds your self-sabotage easy to recognize?

Somebody else! Although it is often easy to identify self-sabotage , our friends and relatives, you are frequently blind to the devious workings of your own self-sabotage mechanism.

2   When is the self-sabotage mechanism at work, and not at work?

It's at work all the time. So when you're awake, it's awake.

Once you know it is always working you begin to see it more clearly. In order to see the ssm at work, you must stop blaming others, stop blaming your circumstances, and take responsibility for the consequences of all your actions.

3   Why does the self-sabotage mechanism do what it does?

To give you undesirable experiences. Why? To make an experience truly meaningful, you need to experience it from all angles.

4   What is true about every action?

It has a consequence. You can't escape the consequence. All actions have consequences, and some consequences are more desirable than others.

5   How does the ssm work?

It's both a master of deception as well as incredibly devious. It rejects truth and aims to label it as false. It will do all it can to persuade you to see what's not really there, and to deceive you into seeing aspects of reality as a falsehood.

Questions and Answers 2.2

1   When you start becoming aware of the self-sabotage mechanism, what happens?

The ssm will step up its efforts to ruin your progress.

2   What enables you to create what you really want for the future?

Change. If you don't change, your circumstances will remain the same. It is only by changing that you are able to create any change in the future. So the ssm acts to resist any and all change!

3   Why can a new perspective evoke feelings of irritation and doubt?

Because the ssm is at work telling you that the new perspective is wrong. Once you realize this thought itself is sabotage, you can open your mind to the new viewpoint and move past the obstacle the ssm has so cunningly tried to create.

4   Do you need to personally experience all the negative as well as the positive aspects of life yourself?

No. You can learn vicariously through the mistakes of others. By reading this book and answering all these questions, you will learn some of the tricks of the ssm and how to overcome them without needing to experience the resultant pain or discomfort yourself.

Questions and Answers 2.3

1   What causes some people to feel a little stressed by reading the ideas presented in this book?

The ssm is trying to subvert the positive effects that learning about its strategies brings you.

2   How is each and every new perspective different?

Each new perspective provides you with a new way of looking at a situation. When fully integrated, each and every one gives you a different amount of personal power.

3   Who always wins by exploring a new perspective?

You do. Once you are finished exploring, you can go back to your old position, if appropriate! Since your open-mindedness may lead you to something new, how can you lose?

4   Are there different ways of looking at any situation in life?

Yes. Many different viewpoints exist for any situation in life. Everyone who disagrees with you usually just has a different perspective on the situation.

5 What does the ssm say about any perspective you don't agree with?

The ssm will say that any perspective you don't agree with is wrong. It will say the same about any viewpoint you don't yet understand. What a deliciously awful way of closing your mind to the extra power a new perspective can give you.

Questions and Answers 2.4

1 How does increasing your awareness help in life?

You start learning to recognize what's actually happening, to avoid the ssm's more blatant strategies, and begin to see some of its more subtle ones.

2 What is the point of learning to anticipate, to become aware of, and to cope better with the ssm?

By avoiding the actions encouraged by the ssm, you stay more in control of your life - which tends to produce more desirable circumstances.

3 Whenever you reach an undesirable consequence, what can you usually say is true?

You've sabotaged yourself in following the ssm's direction to do what doesn't work.

How do you know what doesn't work? Retrospectively, it's very simple - you don't have the results you wanted! And to know in advance is just as simple - don't let the ssm influence your choices...

4 How do you know when the ssm is involved?

When you don't have what you really want, the ssm has been involved. If you're not enjoying a particular moment, the ssm has been involved in some manner or other.

5 In what way does the Alvin Toffler quote relate to the ssm as described here?

Illiteracy no longer just describes to those who can not read and write, but also encompasses those who decline to be open minded enough to learn from another perspective. People who are unable to learn, unlearn, and relearn do not change. Not because they can't change, but because they won't.

If you refuse to evolve along with life, life just evolves without you. You get left behind. And nothing changes in your life!

Questions and Answers 2.5

1   When you've made a mistake, what is probably true of your thoughts?

You've usually done what you thought was right even though it later proved to be wrong. Why? The self-sabotage mechanism can hijack your thinking, and untrue thoughts usually lead to mistaken actions.

2   Who benefits when you evaluate your mistakes?

You do. By evaluating your mistakes you learn that some of your thoughts are simply untrue, which means your thinking can be unreliable. This potent realization takes power away from the ssm.

3   Why Is it fundamental to evaluate each and every thought?

Only by evaluating each thought can you establish the truth or untruth of each and every one. This leads you to more effective actions which then give more desirable consequences. Result? You have more desirable circumstances!

When you think for yourself and learn to integrate new perspectives with your current perspectives, you stop being so gullible. You are no longer at the mercy of other influences. How do you know if they do actually have your best interests at heart?

"They" say that someone is always in control of you life - so it might as well be you!

· - - - - - - · - - - - - - - · - - - - - - · - - - - - ·

Questions and Answers 3

Questions and Answers 3.1

1   *Do your thoughts always tell you the truth?*

Sometimes they do, sometimes they don't. So no, not always.

2   *When do your thoughts not tell you the truth?*

When your self-sabotage mechanism has hijacked the mind to mislead you.

Whenever you are making progress, the ssm will try and prevent you. It often does its job by being negative, so the critical thoughts, the stressful ones, are the ones that are especially important to question.

3   *How do you ascertain if a thought is true or not?*

Investigation!

Use your common sense, is it credible? Does it agree with what else you know to be true? Does it actually make reasonable sense? Is it giving you the results it "should" give you? Will it empower you?

Don't believe any of your thoughts without questioning, without any attempt to determine their truthfulness. The negative ones are more liable to be untrue.

4   *Who decides whether or not you think a thought?*

Thoughts just come and go, presented in a constant stream. Most people just obey their habitual impulse and think them all.

So no, most of your thinking is not under your conscious control. The ssm frequently chooses your thoughts.

5   *If your last answer was, 'Me, I do!' then what makes you think that? Can you choose not to think a thought?*

It's simple to tell if you determine your thinking. Can you stop thinking if you so choose?

If you can cease all thinking at will, then you control your thoughts. If you cannot do so for more than a few seconds, then obviously you don't.

Has your mind ever gone round and round in circles, perhaps when you're trying to sleep? "He said this, which wasn't true, and missed out on the other, which was significant. This was unfair, and he said nothing about that..."

Most people actually have very little control over their thoughts. Believing that you yourself determine your thinking is, by and large, a fallacy, yet one well-loved by the ssm.

Questions and Answers 3.2

1   What's the common misunderstanding about simple and easy?

Most people think that simple means easy. Yet this is just not so.

There's no correlation between the two. Some simple tasks are easy, and some are extremely difficult.

2   How does the story about quitting smoking affect your understanding of simple and easy?

Smoking is a behavior that many smokers know does not work for them. This realization is both simple and "relatively" easy.

However, stopping this unhealthy behavior can be very difficult, even though it is extremely simple.

3   Why are gym memberships affordable, relatively speaking?

Because people don't understand the lack of correlation between simple and easy. Gyms would be a lot more expensive, or go out of business, if they did.

4   What strategy does work to stop smoking?

What works is a two-part strategy. First to choose what you do want rather than what you don't. Put your energy into what you want, good health, rather than into the negative, stopping smoking. See the Focus Principle - the Law of Attraction part Two, in Chapter Four.

With this change in focus, then following through with the single oh-so-simple action necessary becomes less difficult.

5   Why does choosing to do something rather than having to do it make a difference?

When it is your choice, you have chosen to do it, there's no longer a "should".

Then you don't waste your energy complaining about what you're doing, the time it takes, or the other opportunities you might be missing while you are performing the task. Choosing to do something brings calmness into what may be a trying experience, thus making you more effective. The energy released by the let-go is now available to complete the task.

Note the gain in continuing to choose the same thing when faced with the consequences of a previous choice. A child is a (minimum) eighteen year commitment. So your decision years ago to bring up a child is also a choice to look after that child until it's eighteen. This was your choice even though you may have made it implicitly.

Questions and Answers 3.3

1   *What is the difference between real knowing and just knowing about something?*

Knowing about something means you have received the knowledge from the outside. Often people just regurgitate what they've been told rather than their own authentic experience. Then what you understand is third-hand at best.

Much of the world seems to think that listening to what you've heard is the equivalent of having your own experience. Yet without the inner experiencing, you can only know about it. There's little personal power when you know about, even though you understand.

Real knowing comes from experience. You cannot delegate the time and energy. The effort is yours. The more energy you put in, either into your own experiences or vicariously reliving other people's, the more mistakes you can avoid, although you may insist on making your own!

2   *Who is the only one who can give you an experience?*

You! Experience cannot be delegated. You have to put in the time yourself. You must invest your energy to gain the knowledge and experience. Watching TV or reading a book on golf does not make you an expert golfer, which is not to say that reading the words of an expert can't help you improve.

The local TV sports network once advertised itself as the most authentic experience possible! But it's difficult to think of a more misleading assertion. Totally mendacious. If you're not crystal clear here, watch a broadcast of a marathon, then go out and try to run one. Actually doing it yourself is authentic - a totally different experience!

3   How do you know if you really know?

When you really know, you do it as and when appropriate. If you know how to ride a bike, when it comes time to ride one you just get on and ride. You already have the experience, you just do it.

It's also true that if you do not do something at the appropriate time you do not know it. Although, you may indeed know about it.

For example, quitting smoking. See If It's Simple, It Must Be Easy, in Chapter Three. If you are a smoker, you may say you know you need to quit smoking as you light a cigarette. But this just demonstrates the confusion, if you did know right now, you would quit. You may know about quitting, but you don't really know, or you wouldn't still be smoking..

4   Why is failure valuable?

FAIL could be an acronym for First Attempts In Learning. Learning a process, and finding out what doesn't work is just as relevant as finding out what does. When you know that failure is just a mistake, just missing the mark, you are able to move on with the attitude that you've now found out something valuable - something else that doesn't work.

To err is just part of the process. It is indeed human. When you discard everything that doesn't work, you are then left with what does. The learning process consists of being wrong as well as right.

5   What other benefits come when you know that time and energy is essential for authentic knowing?

When you know that real knowing takes real experience, you are aware that your effort is needed. An authentic experience takes time and energy! It's just what is necessary, can't be delegated. This makes it easier for you to invest the required effort.

Many people think they know - although they don't - because they confound understanding and real knowing. When you know someone lacks the experience and the personal power that comes with experience, then failure is highly possible. Not a problem, they just haven't failed enough yet!

So it pays to avoid all situations where there's no alternative. You need to be able to go elsewhere when there's a failure. No options to turn to when somebody - or a company - fails can be very stressful.

This caution applies particularly to monopoly suppliers, especially to government mandated monopolies! What happens when the people involved make the inevitable mistakes? Assuming that someone else is infallible is yet more self-sabotage. It definitely leads to undesirable results.

Questions and Answers 3.4

1   What is your Most Important Question? When do you ask it?

Your Most Important Question is the one that you ask yourself most of the time. It's your choice of the four possibilities listed. It's not the same for everyone. You get to choose your Most Important Question. And you can't make a mistake!

In each specific circumstance, your actions answer an unspoken question. This is your Most Important Question. In advance, you need to make a conscious choice for your default Most Important Question to cover situations in general. Otherwise the ssm will choose it for you...

2   Why is it essential to determine your Most Important Question?

This gets you thinking about the future. The results of your actions.

3   Can you change your Most Important Question having once set it in general?

Yes, of course. As it's general, you may wish to change it as you change. Your Most Important Question may also be varied to suit the circumstance in particular.

Yet you need to remember there are always consequences, though the self-sabotage mechanism will try very, very hard to get you to ignore this vital realization.

4   What are the results of choosing each option as your Most Important Question.

Very good question! Let's investigate each one in turn.

a   "Do I feel like doing it?"

You'll feel good/better right now. Of course, that doesn't say how long that good feeling will last. Sometimes it doesn't last very long, and then you know you've given yourself the wrong answer. Other times, you'll come to a circumstance that's undesirable.

Then you will have decided it was the wrong answer after all. Only you can decide what are the right and wrong answers for you...

Yet be aware how many people in our society presume that they know better than you how you should run your life. Although, as an uninvestigated assumption, this is simply untrue.

As an adult, and we're not addressing children here, only you can decide. No one else can. Then you will live with the consequences of your choices. The freedom to make your own mistakes is an indispensable component of freedom. Without it, freedom is not real freedom.

b   "Do I want to do it?"

Ditto.

c   "Is it me?"

Ditto.

d   "Do I want the results that doing it will bring?"

The actions this choice lead to may be uncomfortable. Perhaps very challenging. Yet you'll be more successful, feel more satisfaction as you move toward your goal, toward more desirable circumstances.

5   *How does determining your general Most Important Question help you?*

Contemplating your general Most Important Question, the one for any circumstance, gets you putting time and energy into the results you desire. Any feelings of resistance as you reflect here tell you that the ssm is trying to negatively impact your choice. Yet you're not answering for the ssm, you want the most significant answer for you.

All actions have consequences, and some consequences are more desirable than others. Different Most Important Questions have different consequences, which result in different circumstances, as Henry realized here.

Questions and Answers 3.5

1   *What happens when you do what works?*

You tend to get the result you desire.

2   *What happens when you do what doesn't work?*

You don't get the result you're looking for.

You realize the consequences of your actions are undesirable.

Your circumstances are not in harmony with whatever you want to be, do, or have.

[These three answers all mean more or less the same here.]

3 How can you tell what does and doesn't work for you?

What works for you is what brings you the results you're looking for. Then your circumstances become more desirable.

If you're not getting the results you desire, or you're not achieving what you want, then you are not doing what works for you.

4 When you're doing what doesn't work for you, what do you do?

When in a hole - stop digging! You'll never regret this later.

There are several choices. Assuming that you do really want what you think you want, then you need to do something differently, to do it some other way. You need to assess the effectiveness of what you are doing, which requires accurate knowledge of your goal. You may even need to redefine your goal.

One indispensable choice you need to make is to explicitly choose to do it, rather than do it because you think you have to do it. There are no have-to's in life, although there are indeed very difficult choices, arduous situations, and very undesirable consequences.

Questions and Answers 3.6

1 What's required to get you to where you want to be?

Change. Without effective change, nothing changes! This means change in you!

2 Who benefits when you change?

You! Effective change increases your personal power, you are the major beneficiary.

Yet unless you have the power to change, you are powerless. Then you cannot change.

This is why it is critical that you take responsibility for yourself. If you say that you are not responsible, you are also saying that you have no power in these circumstances. Taking responsibility for yourself gives you the power to change yourself and your circumstances.

3   Why is it essential for you to become more aware?

Awareness is vital for personal power. If you're unaware of any difference then you're unlikely to be able to make a difference.

4   How does clarity come into it?

Clarity focuses our awareness. Unless you are clear about what specifically will make a difference, then any changes will be random and probably ineffective.

You might get lucky, but why rely on luck? Rather internalize the differences that make the difference. Then their power helps you become more effective. Then you have more control over your own destiny.

5   When are you more effective?

The more you know about what can make a difference, the more effective you are. Then you are aware of what's significant. The clearer you are, the more specific you can be about doing what works in the situation.

Questions and Answers 4

Questions and Answers 4.1

1   Describe the Law of Attraction, part One.

Energy energizes! You attract what you put your energy into, and all energy is creative. This includes your time as well as your energy.

2   What do many people miss here?

Most people miss that the Law of Attraction part One is not qualified, it's absolute. So whatever you put your energy into will increase in your life. No matter what it is!

This statement "No matter what it is" means that it applies equally to the negative as well as to the positive.

Neil visualized losing his clients, his money running out, letting his secretary go... And then it all came to fruition. Fruition is the perfect word here, his business failing was indeed the fruit of his misapplied energy.

Bonus question. What does this law have to do with the increasing levels of violence in the world?

3   When does is it operate?

All of the time. All energy is creative, and helps to produce some effect.

It also attracts situations which enable you to develop any qualities that you wish to improve. So things may seem to get worse. Initially, you may judge such situations as negative, and only later see the positive. Sometimes only years later.

This Law will bring you amazingly appropriate opportunities to change your previous responses to something more beneficial to you in the circumstances.

4   Who does this Law benefit?

It applies to us all, including you!

Yet to benefit, remember that all your energy is creative and use it appropriately, (see the next koan, part Two). To produce positive situations and results you must put energy into the positive, although it may take some time to recognize your benefit in some situations!

5   How do we choose a strategy which works?

Stop reacting to outside circumstances. You need to see when your previous actions - your re-actions - didn't give you the results you desired last time. And are unlikely to do so this time.

Look to see how this circumstance might benefit you - there is always a benefit, even if you don't know what it is yet. My mother used to tell me that every cloud has a silver lining.

Then you can choose to respond more appropriately, which means think first, check that your thoughts are not misleading you, consider all aspects including the likely outcome as well as your feelings, and then act.

Remember the value of an attitude of gratitude.

Questions and Answers 4.2

1   What is the Focus Principle?

It tells you how to apply your energy, to focus on what you do want rather than what you don't. It's the second aspect to the Law of Attraction.

2   How can you tell that Mother Teresa really understood this Principle?

Mother Teresa refused to attend an anti-war march, to put any energy into what she didn't want to energize. In stark contrast, she stated her willingness to attend a march that was pro-peace.

3   Why is this distinction so crucial? Reflect on its impact in society.

It's absolutely basic to understanding many of the problems in our society.

Most of us have no idea of the extent that the Focus Principle contributes to the problems of today. For example, our society has a war against drugs, a war against poverty, a war against terror, a war against... And although we observe these problems getting worse, most people make little attempt to understand the underlying cause. We say we're at war, then we wonder why we're at war!

TV programs often contain much violence, and then we wonder why there's so much violence in our world. And as for love, or rather the scarcity of love...

4   When do we use this Principle to sabotage ourselves?

When we say things like, "I can't afford it." Or, "I can't do that." Or, "I don't have the time." Or, "I'm bad at remembering names."

In our casual conversations, many people play the "ain't it awful" game. And then we profess astonishment at the outcomes our focus and our energy help create!

5   Who might find this Principle difficult to apply?

Those who don't understand that their thoughts could be under their conscious control. The ssm likes to ignore the incredible benefits that such awareness brings.

Most of us make little or no attempt to monitor our thoughts, and when we do, we complain that positive thinking is so difficult. We don't realize that changing our context, which includes our thinking and our attitude, is the most effective game in town. The place to effect any long-lasting and effective change is internally. So start practicing today. Right now!

Questions and Answers 4.3

1   What is the third part of the Law of Attraction?

The Golden Rule. "Do unto others as you would have them do unto you."

As many of us already understand, this means, "What goes around, comes around." Our grandparent's proverb was, "As you sow, so shall you reap." Newton's Third Law of Motion is an instance of this maxim in science.

2   Why is this fundamental?

Because energy energizes - the first part of the Law of Attraction. If you are nice, helpful, considerate to others, the Golden Rule tells us that you'll attract nice, helpful, considerate behaviors from others in the long-term. And the opposite also applies!

3   Who does this rule affect?

All three aspects of the Law of Attraction: Energy Energizes, the Focus Principle, and the Golden Rule apply to everybody all the time. This includes you!

4   What are the implications of the Golden Rule?

For your own sake, only do to someone else what you'd like someone else to do to you. Why? Because, although not necessarily immediately, your actions will come back to you.

This motivation is generally misunderstood by virtually everybody, if not ignored completely. Most people seems to think of the Golden Rule as part of ethics or reciprocity, rather than as the highly practical consequence of an unequivocal Universal Law.

Anything that you think is unfair to you may well be simply the Golden Rule in action, although you may well have forgotten your original part in invoking this. Just as decisively, it explains why revenge is not effective, since it cannot help but perpetuate the problem. Although you may wonder why mankind has not worked this out for itself after so many centuries of experience.

Who is the major beneficiary when you keep it? You yourself. Rather than anyone else, you are the major beneficiary in both the short-term as well as the long-term. So follow the Golden Rule steadfastly!

Questions and Answers 4.4

1   What is the most compelling lesson my mother taught me?

To think for myself, rather than rely on the assertions of others, the reliability of their beliefs, and the accuracy of their thinking.

2   Why is this so valuable?

Thinking for yourself avoids being at the mercy of other people's uninvestigated thinking and beliefs. Rather remain skeptical, don't believe and yet don't disbelieve, instead check out things for yourself.

Anyone who tries to teach you anything is usually just telling you what they believe. Our parents, our educators, our boss, a coworker, friends, etc., rarely know to think it through and convert their belief into real knowing. So even when you know they are sincere in telling you the truth, the whole truth, and nothing but the truth in their view, they may still be sincerely mistaken.

If they don't encourage you to check something out, to think it through for yourself, then are they really interested in you arriving at your truth? Investigation is the most reliable way to avoid being manipulated.

If you assume what they tell you is entirely true, no matter how plausible it may appear, how can you say you really know it? Thorough investigation is needed before what someone else tells you becomes your truth. Otherwise it just remains a belief. And we don't believe in believing, we believe in knowing.

3   *Who is totally responsible for the circumstances of your life?*
Discuss your answer.

You are! And this is wonderful news!

Responsibility brings power. When you take total responsibility for your circumstances, you also give yourself the power to change them. When you say you are not responsible, you lack power, and without power, change is difficult.

It's very empowering to realize that you are 100% responsible for your part in creating your circumstances. This allows you to take total responsibility for the circumstances in your life.

If you put your energy into what you cannot change, then nothing will change! Whereas when you put your energy into changing what you can change, this inevitably benefits your future circumstances.

4   *What is the drawback of believing others? Of believing any belief itself?*

A belief, no matter how plausible, requires energy to become your truth. It may just be an old wives tale that someone still believes. How many people have your interests as their highest priority? Be skeptical rather than gullible or cynical.

Anything that you have not thought through for yourself is not your truth. To arrive at your truth requires your time and your energy. This is why just adopting other people's beliefs gives you little power, and there's so much more power in truth.

Truth is rather like physical fitness, you can't delegate the required work. Power unfolds from within, in the same way that trees grow, in fact as everything in nature grows. So follow the wisdom of nature, do things the way nature does. First invest the time and energy to ensure it is your truth. Then live your truth.

Questions and Answers 4.5

1.   *What is the mistaken but common view of stress illustrated in this koan?*

We often think that stress comes by not being able to drive. But this is just not so . As a child in kindergarten, I couldn't drive, yet this caused me no stress. I was unconscious of my incompetence, which has no stress.

2.   Who finds learning stressful?

Virtually all of us.

Most people find change stressful, because the ssm resists change. So everything that involves change, such as learning a new capability, or even simply becoming more capable, can be stressful.

Stress is normal when you want something, and either you don't have it, or you don't know how to get it. It's the gap between what you want, the need, the craving to drive, and the reality of knowing that you can't that causes much stress, rather than the actual incapacity itself.

3.   When does stress diminish?

When you understand what causes it.

As you saw in this story, stress often goes hand in hand with learning anything new. Rather than anything bad, understand it's just par for the course. Stress is inherent in your attachment to getting the result of whatever you want, your desired outcome. Whether what you want is a thing, or a capability, or a person, or a feeling...

This helps remove the stress involved in such common thoughts as "I shouldn't be stressed," or "it's wrong to be stressed," or "stress is unnatural" etc., etc.

4.   How else can you reduce stress?

Know that other people have achieved the result you want, so you take the view that, "If they can do it, so can I."

Decrease your dissatisfaction of the gap between reality - what is right now - and wherever you think you should be. In any way that works for you.

Reduce your expectations of the results you should be achieving, or should have achieved, by now. In fact, give up all shoulds.

Give yourself more time to achieve, to learn a new capability.

Another good strategy is to chunk down a task to manageable levels, then just focus on the first achievable sub-task. Just forget, for the moment, about the rest of it. Each of these can reduce stress.

• - - - - - • - - - - - - - • - - - - - - - • - - - - - •

Questions and Answers 5

Questions and Answers 5.1

1   When you disagree with someone, and you are sure you are right, does that mean the other must be wrong?

No, not necessarily. Two people will frequently have a different perspective on a matter. So you may be disagreeing about your viewpoint, or your opinion, or your interpretation of what happened, or what's actually relevant. Or about what it means, or what may happen, or the long-term consequences...

2   What can you tell about a disagreement in which you being right does mean that the other person is indeed wrong?

It means you are disagreeing about the facts of the matter, the past, rather than your opinion, your perspective, your understanding, what it means, how to proceed...

The facts about the past are the facts about the past, they do not change. What happened, happened, even though reliable facts can often be difficult to ascertain. Nevertheless, sub-atomic quantum physics notwithstanding, the facts can usually be stated pretty objectively.

3   How are being right and being effective connected? Discuss your answer.

Being right may be very effective, and it may be totally ineffective. They are not connected.

You can be right, and yet your actions will not get you to your goal, even if you know what your goal is. Some people's goal is to enjoy the journey, rather than achieve something in the future.

Conversely, you may not be right from the other person's viewpoint, and yet reach your goal, which means your actions were effective.

4   What does this tell us about being right, and being effective?

It suggests that being right is not that relevant. What is significant is whether the action in question will or will not help you reach your desired goal - is it effective?

This of course means that it's valuable, if not indispensable, to know what you are trying to achieve, what your desired goal is. As well as knowing that your goals may be very different from those of the other person.

5   How does this help us resolve an argument?

If you can look dispassionately at the other person's viewpoint, you will appreciate why you disagree. Your willingness to investigate gives you the big picture. Then you can determine if you differ about the facts, or about your objectives. You may be able to understand why they say what they say. This helps stop you from judging them as wrong, which itself goes a long way toward defusing any disagreement.

Your willingness to be open-minded, to listen carefully to their perspective may also make them more willing to listen to yours.

Summary: The six-part strategy to resolve arguments

1   I'm right does NOT mean you're wrong.

2   Furthermore, being right is actually not what's important anyway. What's important is effectiveness in achieving your goal.

3   Holding onto your current perspective - Being Right, aka Being Righteous - will not allow resolution. This just perpetuates the current situation. You need to understand the other person's viewpoint.

4   To resolve the situation, you need to go and look at the other person's perspective, even though you don't get it - especially when it seems wrong. That movement to understand their perspective is only temporary.

5   Once you've seen and ensured that you understand what they're saying; and let the other person know that you now understand their perspective; you can then go back to your previous position.

6   Then you integrate your new understanding with the old perspective that you already had, combining the best of the old with the best of the new.

           Then they know their perspective have been heard, and you can transcend any limitations in your previous viewpoint.

Questions and Answers 5.2

1   What is the benefit of planning strategies in advance to improve your mood ?

When you are feeling good about yourself, you are more able to think of things that make you feel positive, and you have the energy to plan enjoyable activities in advance. You end up with a longer and more effective list.

But when you are negative it's hard to think of enjoying yourself. And everybody around you may be influenced by your bad mood.

2 Who benefits if you do something enjoyable when you are in a black mood?

You do. When you restore your peace of mind and a positive mood you feel better. Yet you may have to make yourself do it!

Actually, everybody around you benefits when you improve your frame of mind, not just you.

3 Why rely on strategies you can perform solo to improve your state?

Because another person might not be around to make you feel better. That special person might be the reason you're in a bad mood in the first place!

When you can improve your frame of mind on your own, you're more likely to do it! The less you need for a strategy, and the less complex it is, the less it involves. And hence you're more likely to be successful!

4 Which specific strategies could help improve your mood next time you need a lift? Plan ahead now!

Some that work for me are:

Physical exercise. I can focus on working out hard and leave the upset for the moment. Or simply go for a walk. Nature is full of life, the trees, the birds, the wind, and the rain. It is there to be enjoyed, it lifts my spirit.

Reading something. I like Richard Bach's Jonathan Livingston Seagull, for example. I've read it so often, it only takes me twenty minutes to reread the whole book, and it always improves my mood. I find Osho also has a great deal to offer.

Reciting something. For example, I love Shakespeare's sonnets. Since the language is so archaic, they took a while to really appreciate, but learning them by heart has enabled me to really get to know their amazing value. I love #29, "When in disgrace with fortune and men's eyes." Another favorite is #148, 'Oh me, what eyes hath love put in my head", for when love doesn't cooperate. Then there's the timeless beauty of #18, 'Shall I compare thee to a summer's day?"

"When in Disgrace" so brilliantly captures the essential spirit of a black mood that I'm left in awe how well Shakespeare reaches out across the centuries to demonstrate exactly how we feel.

Listening to music. I love opera and classical music. Mozart does lots for me.

Singing something. Two of my favorites are: 'Dear Lord and Father of Mankind," a Christian hymn. And the "Prayer of St. Francis" is even more wonderful vocally than it is in prose.

Friends can help me get out of a black mood. So if I'm feeling down, I always accept all and any invitations to go out. Company does help!

Analyzing the situation. Sometimes I think to ask myself, what could be the cause? Then I write down the answer that comes, and explore, investigate it. This can work.

Leaving the problem aside for now, and just doing something else, anything, can sometimes be helpful.

Work. As mentioned in the earlier koan, "Since I'm right, you must be wrong!", I've found that hard work can also take you away from a black mood. Although working non-stop for three months is not exactly a short-term strategy, I agree.

Questions and Answers 5.3

1   What is usually true when you say someone "should" have done something?

You think someone "should" because, in fact, they have not done it.

So you are arguing with reality. Socrates' dictum is that people do what they think is right. But you disagree, you think they should have done something that they didn't do.

The same is true of a "should-not." Then they did something, and you think they should not have done it. You're still arguing with reality.

2   When you think someone else is wrong, who does this create stress or pain for?

It is usually more painful for you than for them. Your ssm has hijacked your thoughts once again and then you stress and experience internal conflict about what's wrong. There's far less stress about what you think is right.

Sometimes they won't even know your opinion, and may be completely at ease with the situation. On the other hand, even if you don't tell them explicitly, they may react negatively when they realize you think they "should" have.

3   How effective is the strategy of letting someone else know that they are wrong?

Most people like being right. So they will often turn the tables and make you wrong in return. Or simply write you out of their life because they don't like your negativity.

Hence it's generally not very successful. Why is this so? I hear you ask. Such a good question, let's explore the reasons.

In Chapter Four, part One to the Law of Attraction, Energy Energizes, tells you that no matter what you put your energy into, it will increase. Here, you're putting your energy into being wrong. So wrong behavior increases.

Then part Two is the Focus principle. You're putting your focus on what you don't want - wrong behavior, others being wrong - rather than what you do want. And then what you don't want increases. You will experience even more unwanted behavior.

The Golden Rule is part Three. What you do to others will be done unto you. So if you see other people are behaving wrongly, then other people will do the same and also see you as behaving wrongly!

So this strategy energizes wrong behavior, increases others being wrong in your eyes, and ensures other people will make you wrong in return! It uses all three parts of the Law of Attraction against you. No wonder making someone wrong is generally ineffective!

4   But what if they really are wrong?

How do you know they really are wrong? They think they are right, they disagree. Unless you are discussing the past, the facts and only the facts, isn't this just your opinion?

But okay, let's be generous and instead assume this is actually a very valid assessment. Yet do you know what they're trying to achieve, for sure ?

Even they may not know what they're really trying to achieve, since the ssm may have hijacked their thoughts and got them to adopt one of its goals instead...

Can you be absolutely sure you do know? Yet notice that making them wrong doesn't make you feel good about them. So what this tells us is that the ssm has hijacked your thinking process, and got you to judge them. And judging, making someone wrong, rarely works; see the answer to the previous question immediately above.

5   *Explore the shoulds and the should-nots that you have in your life. Which do you hold for yourself and about others? Write them down for your own private use.*

You may already know which shoulds and should-nots are producing desirable results, and which ones are not. Then you can explore them all in order to let the ineffective ones go. Letting go of those that don't serve you will make you more effective, no matter what you do.

Questions and Answers 5.4

1   *What does this story tell us about being negative?*

Everything has a consequence, an outcome is both inevitable, and inescapable. And negative behavior has negative consequences, it lessens the desirability of the outcome. This means that the consequence is not as good as it would be without the negativity, rather than the outcome is not good at all.

2.   *Who lost out from my negativity, my disgruntling?*

We all did. But I lost the most. The desired motivation - the whole point of the evening - was not achieved. Once again we see the deleterious effect of being negative.

3   *How can we refer to negative behavior or circumstances without invoking the Law of Attraction to perpetuate them.*

By using the phrase "Up till now, I used to..." As in, "Up till now, I used to insist I didn't have the time." Or, "Up till now, I knew I couldn't afford it." Or, "Up till now, they/it used to annoy me."

This places the undesirable behavior in the past, which avoids giving it any energy in the present.

4.   *What other benefits does being positive about the negative have?*

The phrase "Up till now ..." suggests that although this used to be what happened in the past, from now on things will be different. It stops the past from being perpetuated into the future. This is exactly what you want when talking about the negative!

Questions and Answers 6

Questions and Answers 6.1

1   What does this koan tell you about your mind?

That the mind can override your wishes. Or, more precisely, that the ssm can get you to do what it wants by hijacking your mind. Which suggests that you and your mind are not the same thing!

As you saw in the story, the ssm got me to say something - anything - despite explicit instructions not to.

2   Which of the two wolves is your self-sabotage mechanism?

Black reflects darkness, while white represents light. The black wolf attempts to sabotage your progress. And it doesn't just speak, it insists, it snaps and snarls, and can even get you to emote furiously with powerful, sometimes even totally uncalled for emotions.

3   How does each wolf get stronger?

With energy. You give a wolf energy when you listen to it. When you find value in what it says. When you pay attention to its blandishments. When you follow its suggestions.

So only give energy to the white wolf! Simple, but simple does not necessarily mean easy!

Questions and Answers 6.2

1.   What does this koan tell you about something that appears to be free?

You have not yet realized what its price is, or are overlooking something about it. Everything has a price and although you may not have to pay the price immediately, eventually, you will.

2.   Does this mean that there are always consequences?

Yes indeed, there are consequences to everything you do, and everything you don't do. Even if you do nothing, there's still an outcome. No exceptions.

The time and energy you expend for those future consequences, in one view, is the price. A powerful way of looking at money is that it's simply a useful way of storing time and energy for the future. Which suggests that once you have enough money for the future, then putting additional effort into acquiring even more is simply an unnecessary waste of your time and energy.

3.   *How do you benefit by paying the price now?*

Like at a bank, you benefit by paying the charges sooner, since the price becomes higher as the delay gets longer. Banks charge interest, although people are not necessarily charged on the same scale. Your circumstances determine how you are charged.

Life operates in a similar manner. The longer you wait, the more you will pay, although again different for each person. Life assesses your own unique fee, and fees increases as time passes.

You gain in another way when you complete something now. When left unfinished, it hangs around consuming both current and future time and energy. Handled immediately, no more action is needed, it's now complete. Complete is good because it allows you more freedom to move on.

Questions and Answers 6.3

1   *What are temptations and distractions?*

They are diversions by the ssm that prevent us from achieving what we've set out to achieve. Attempts to sabotage what could really serve us...

The closer you come to your goal, the more the ssm may try to distract you. Since its job is to give you what you don't really want, it may try harder, perhaps by presenting you with negative emotions and/or misleading thoughts. Be forewarned, emoting can be incredibly distracting!

2   *When we allow ourselves to be distracted or tempted, what happens?*

Nothing much changes. We continue to repeat the past, our goals are deferred, and we just get More Of The Same.

The ssm is inherently deceitful. A temptation tries to sway us from something desirable by misleading us toward something apparently more desirable. Yet all changes in direction take time and energy. With continual changes, we tend to remain exactly where we are now.

It also tries to distract us from something not particularly desirable by suggesting we do something else a bit less undesirable. Again, we tend to end up with More Of The Same.

3   How best to cope with temptations and distractions?

Just see them for what they really are. Attempts by the black wolf to divert you from your goals. If you change direction often enough, nothing really changes and you stay where you are.

First decide where you really want to be, and don't allow any digressions from your plan to get there. Plan your work, then work your plan!

The more that temptations and distractions come up, the more the ssm is trying to divert you from your goal. So the closer your goal becomes, the harder the black wolf will try. The more stressful you find its snapping and snarling at what you're learning here, the more reassurance you have that you're on track!

Questions and Answers 6.4

1   What is true about frustration?

It clearly informs you that changes need to be made. The powerful question to ask here is: Where?

The ssm will give you the answer that external changes are the way to go, but the real benefit is when you change. This means changing your internal perspective, your context.

2   Who has to change to relieve your frustration?

You can wish for the situation to change, but how often do any changes suit you in an enduring fashion?

It's your frustration, and it's inside your head, so that's where you need to make changes. The other person doesn't need to. Donald chose not to, and so didn't benefit.

Only one person has to change to stop their part in a disagreement. Notice that you can stop disagreeing, and yet the other person may insist on continuing. This can be very funny, while enormously frustrating for the other.

3   *How can you use frustration to benefit you?*

You benefit when you use frustration constructively, i.e. make the internal changes indicated. Frustration is energy, negative energy which feeds the black wolf, the ssm, see the koan The Wolves - an American Indian viewpoint, earlier in this chapter.

You can't necessarily change what's outside, but you can change your understanding. You can use frustration as motivation to find out how things look from the other side. To explore why the other person thinks they're right.

Your context, your perspective, is the only thing you have any real control over. If you learn to manage your thoughts the same way you manage your actions, your emotions will also change. Rather feed the white wolf. Then you're no longer frustrated, and can have fun instead.

4   *Discuss Donald's ssm in the story.*

His ssm stopped him seeing another viewpoint and kept him from getting what he really wanted - my cooperation. He was so worked up in frustration that when I did finally tell him I understood his viewpoint, he couldn't hear it. Even when he did, it set him so off balance, he didn't enjoy being right. His ssm did a deliciously dreadful job.

Questions and Answers 6.5

1.   *What is your intuition?*

Your intuition is your inner knowing, your inner vibe, sometimes called the still small voice of calm. Intuition can be seen as two words, in-tuition. This offers sure guidance, and yet never minds if you ignore it.

It's generally drowned out in all the commotion when the ssm has hijacked your mind, is emoting, or shouting at you. Yet if you can stop to listen closely enough, it's that little voice of calm, sage wisdom you hear sometimes.

2.   *When are you most effective?*

Whenever you can observe from a place of calm and clarity, which means the ssm is no longer trying to run the show at that moment. Don't worry, it'll be back shortly!

From this place we just know what needs to be done and we handle it. It's easier to think rationally when the ssm hasn't hijacked the mind.

3.   How will you know when the self-sabotage mechanism is no longer in complete charge?

One minute you'll have peace and calm, then the ssm will again be trying to run your life. Remember, it doesn't know how to have fun. Success usually comes incrementally, in small stages. The more you've been feeding the black wolf, the stronger it is and the more food it wants.

Each moment will be different. You may feel life becomes a yo-yo as the black wolf snaps and snarls. Persist anyway, it may be tough, but you never give yourself situations you can't handle. Overcoming the black wolf is actually the only real game in town.

With more peace, you can get things done, you're more effective. You become more able to handle things calmly. Calmness brings clarity, even as others are losing their heads, even in situations where you might previously have stressed. You have more fun, and life becomes more enjoyable. Congratulations!

I've heard that when you've overcome the ssm completely, you can walk on water!

• - - - - - - • - - - - - - • - - - - - - • - - - - - •

Questions and Answers 7

Questions and Answers 7.1

1. *Why can running at redline be detrimental?*

Running at redline creates serious stress. The redline point indicates when the engine is working at its maximum. Work it any harder, and it over-stresses, which is just asking for trouble.

There's nothing wrong with stress from time to time, some stress is beneficial. Yet everything in moderation. Breakdowns come whenever anything is over-stressed. Over-stressing comes in two flavors: the first is too much stress at any one point; and the second is high but acceptable stress for too long, which means trying to run close to redline most of the time. Either of these may apply to you!

When running at redline there's little time to enjoy the journey - you're too busy working. In today's high pressure society, it's easy to forget that to enjoy life involves enjoying the journey. The scenery is also there to be enjoyed.

2. *Is it possible to have too much of a good thing?*

Hmmm. Good question! Maybe yes, maybe no. Does it come without undue effort? The words to focus on here are "too much." If having it creates too much hassle, means too much running around, involves too many people, takes too much energy, consumes too much time, swallows too much whatever, then it probably is too much.

3. *Is it possible to do too much of a good thing?*

Yes indeed. Unequivocally.

The ssm often interprets the original question above, "Can you have too much of a good thing?" to mean "Can you do too much of a good thing?"

But a decision in advance for every moment in the future just takes away your freedom when the future gets here. Rather give yourself some space to decide in the moment. They say there is only now, the eternal moment of now. I've heard that yesterday is just a memory and tomorrow is simply a speculation.

Yet when something is desirable, you tend to want to indulge. Although it's natural to want to squeeze the maximum out of life, remember that less is sometimes more.

The ssm fails to recognize that enough and too much are two very different things. So the answer to this remarkably incisive question is a resounding yes!

4.   *When do you have true freedom?*

When you are free to do what you want to do when you want to do it. Which includes the freedom to do nothing when that choice feels right. Everyone needs down-time; not just the enforced down-time known as sleep. Running at redline most of the time is not sustainable in the long run.

The ssm's job is sabotage. Which means it'll try to get you to believe this is urgent, you must do that, you've got to do the other, everything is important, you gotta, gotta, gotta...

Yet when the ssm has you believing that everything is urgent, this just means nothing is urgent!

True freedom comes from discipline. Self-discipline. Discipline over what you think you should do. But this means what you think rather than what the ssm thinks! Freedom comes with control over your internal landscape. Your context makes the difference!

5.   *If you're running at redline now, what are some of the fundamental questions that you may not have asked yourself, or whose answers you may be ignoring?*

Once you've created your questions, it doesn't matter in which order you answer them, provided you remember every one, any order is fine.

Since your current answers may have been given by the ssm, when you have an answer, investigate it, reflect on it. Is it your true answer? Or has the ssm hijacked your thoughts again? Whenever any of this feels stressful, that stress tells you the ssm is getting involved right now.

For your life in general, ask yourself the following questions:

- What do you want to accomplish with your life long-term? And right now?

- Who is important in your life? Your business activities? yourself? your family? your wife? your kids? your friends?

- Which parts of your current life are you enjoying? Which parts do you not?

- Why are you doing the parts that you don't enjoy?

- If you're living your dream life, is it really your dream life? Or is it actually the ssm's version of your dream life? Or your parent's, or your spouse's?

For your current activities, ask yourself:

- What do you spend your time doing?

- Why are you so very busy?

- When do you have time for yourself alone?

- Do you really need the results or the income that each current activity brings?

- What else could you do with the time this takes? And would that change make your life more or less enjoyable?

- How much time do you currently spend with each important category on a regular basis? Will that time allocation will bring you the results you want?

- How much unscheduled time do you have each day to be spontaneous? This is time for you. Do you give yourself the time to enjoy impromptu activities?

For each possible future opportunity, ask:

- What are you going to give up to find the time it will take?

- Why are you considering spending the time it'll take?

- Have you questioned your mind when it tells you that you need the extra income, or the different results that you'll have?

- Can you afford the time it will take?

- How well will you manage without the results it would bring?

- How will you cope with the consequences of giving up what you'll need to give up to make time for it?

- Will this add or subtract from your enjoyment of life?

For each answer, reflect on whether it satisfies you. If your answers do not, plan the changes that will bring you more enjoyment, then carry out that plan. Remember that keeping your word is absolutely vital. They say that your integrity is all you really have long-term, so keep both the letter and the spirit of each and every current commitment. Consider all and any new commitments very, very carefully.

Questions and Answers 7.2

1.   *What does the scientific method have to do with doubt?*

The scientific method is all about doubt, which is suspension of belief rather than disbelief. You begin with doubt, and you continue to doubt until such time as your doubts have disappeared. Then instead you know.

Through investigation, trial and error, research, and experiments, scientists test theories, hypotheses and speculations until they are either proven or disproven. This is the skeptical position: neither to believe nor to disbelieve, rather to check it out for yourself.

You benefit hugely when you use this process to check validity for yourself. Until such time as you know something to be true, continue to research and investigate, just as the scientist does. Then you're neither being gullible, nor cynical. Rather be skeptical and avoid being manipulated, then you can't be taken advantage of.

2.   Discuss the two types of doubt. How do they differ?

Doubt about what happened on the outside, how things are, the external truth, the facts. And doubt about the inside, your thoughts, your beliefs, what something means to you, your truth.

Initially, all doubt is productive. Doubt stops you being gullible, being taken advantage of. Remember that you only know once you've checked it out, until then it's only a belief.

So start off by doubting what people tell you. Doubt what you hear has happened, what people tell you are the facts and their causes, how things are, and why things have happened. What other people tell you is usually second-hand at least, so for you their beliefs are third-hand at best!

This acknowledgment that we don't have the whole story motivates us to continue to looking. Living in the question is healthy. Yet once you know the facts, doubt stops being effective and becomes counterproductive. Doubt then just wastes your time and energy.

Treat your internal world just the same. Also start off by doubting what your ssm tells you. Doubt your thoughts, doubt your beliefs, doubt what something means to you, doubt your conclusions, doubt yourself. Until you've investigated internally, until you've checked a thought out for yourself, how do you know if it's your truth? Might it be just more of the ssm's sabotage?

3.   Why does the ssm want you to doubt?

The ssm's job is to sabotage you, it wants your energy.

When you know something to be true, your ssm will do all it can to stop you benefitting from the power inherent in that truth. So trust yourself. Once you have investigated, and have come to the point where you know something to be your truth, it is time to cast all doubt aside and trust what you now know. Ignore all the ssm's attempts at persuasion, tell it to go away and leave you alone! Remember you have taken the time to investigate, that's how you know!

The ssm wants you to be uncertain, to question what you know. It lives on the juice, the energy you put into believing and acting on its thoughts. When you allow yourself to doubt your already investigated thoughts you are feeding the black wolf. Rather stay true what you've worked hard to know is true, stay true to yourself.

4. What's so funny about the ssm's use of doubt?

It says, "Believe me, and doubt yourself." And this story demonstrates what can happen when you believe the ssm!

The ssm wants you to trust it, to believe everything it tells you without question. Yet at the same time it wants to doubt your own truth; to doubt the conclusion of your investigations; to doubt despite the time and energy you've invested in ascertaining the facts; to doubt your experiences; basically, to doubt your own self.

• - - - - - - • - - - - - - - • - - - - - - • - - - - - •

9 SOME FINAL DETAILS

9.1   About the author

Born at a very early age, Cris Baker grew up in England where he eventually learned to ride his brother's red bicycle. Fortunately, the family had no TV, and the family's evening pastime was reading. His sister enjoyed Regency romances, and so these, too, got read along with everything else, including much science fiction and fantasy.

Robert Heinlein was a favorite author, and his masterpiece, Stranger in a Strange Land, made an enormous impression. This book undoubtedly influenced his early desire to learn to create life exactly the way he wants it.

After starting out in the special honors Mathematics program at University, the highest level available, a not particularly successful stint saw him graduate with a pass degree - the lowest. Apparently if you stick it out for the full three years, they think you deserve at least some sort of recognition. Although he got much practice at contract bridge, snooker, judo, and repairing his motorcycle, for some reason his accomplishments in these demanding pastimes were not recognized by the authorities.

Close to three decades ago, when he saw a pattern of non-accomplishment, of successive failure begin to emerge, he decided to attend at least one personal growth event each year. And for most of the past thirty years, he has been on more than one such growth experience. One of the first was Mind Dynamics with Alexander Everett. You may know Alexander as one of Werner Erhard's teachers. When visiting Alexander at his farm in Oregon some years later, he mentioned that when he had ceased his involvement with Mind Dynamics, he gave away his dozen or so training centers to his center managers across the world. In California, that center evolved into est (Erhard Seminar Training), which then morphed into one of the more successful entrants in the human potential movement.

Many valuable lessons were also gained from several Money and You courses conducted by Robert Kiyosaki, of Rich Dad, Poor Dad fame. The teaching style was innovative, and the courses enormously experiential. In fact, that experiential aspect was one of the motivations to base this book on the experiences of the author. The major difference being that Robert's courses focused on successful experiences, while this is largely based on the failures!

Marriage was very instructive, there was much to learn. And he obviously learned at least something since he's still friends with his ex-wife. He still recognizes her many good qualities and was delighted to receive an enormous compliment recently when she told him that, "Getting married to you was the best thing that has happened in my life." Among the many, many failures there was at least one success.

The computer industry was relatively kind to him. Eventually he had a lot of success in his own computer company in Canada. The company specialized in performance, teaching people how to get their computers to perform more effectively. Even though it was his own company, this job eventually disappeared when the Americans viewed Canada as far too lucrative a territory for a highly-paid distributor.

So he retired for a few years in South Africa, and then decided to market his vast experience in failure. If you know of the success of the outsourcing industry, then this has to be a winner, right? Who in their right mind would choose to have the experience of failing themselves when they can delegate the job, and learn the same lessons from an expert? Rather avoid the trauma and pain of actually having those experiences!

Yet his education did make some sort of impression. Along the way, he learned the phrase, "Those who can, do. Those who can't, teach." With so much experience in finding out that he cannot do, he decided to go into teaching. Hence this book. Don't worry, this is only a brief introduction to self-sabotage, there are lots more practical experiences to write about...

. - - - - - . - - - - - .

Yet before I let you go, my editor, Debbie, says I should tell you a little bit more about me and what I do. So for those who like to know such things, here goes:

For the last few months, I seem to have done nothing else but spend time writing this book, editing this book, rewriting this book, clarifying questions and answers for this book, moving stuff around in this book, and doing other things to this book. So I hope y'all appreciate the hard work...

What do I do when I'm not reading or writing? I go to gym fairly regularly, I enjoy music, spending time with friends, Formula One motor-racing is a passion, and I eat and sleep. And since I want what I want, and I enjoy enjoying myself, I continue to put a lot of effort into finding out what works. Which all too often means experiencing what doesn't work first. Clients benefit by learning strategies proven by experience, rather than needing to go through all the failures themselves...

How am I like my readers? I hope you're not too much like me! I sometimes wonder if I'm a glutton for punishment. Failure can be painful and, as you have seen, I have lots, lots of experience in that area!

• - - - - - • - - - - - - - - • - - - - - - • - - - - - •

9.2   How to contact us

Our website is:

www.LifeStrategies.net

Our email address is:

teamssm1@LifeStrategies.net

Our office hours are 10 am to 4 pm Central European Time, GMT +0200, and our telephone number is:

+350-200-71-697, please leave a message if we're not available.

However, for the fastest response, all support and billing related questions should be emailed to **teamssm1@LifeStrategies.net.** Any telephone request will take longer to receive a reply because it will need to be manually forwarded to the correct department.

Our physical address is:

#8c - 29 City Mill Lane, Gibraltar 646, Europe

CPSIA information can be obtained
at www.ICGtesting.com
Printed in the USA
FSOW03n0508090516
20215FS